Mary Elizabeth Osborn

COLLECTED POEMS

HENRY TREECE

FROM A PAINTING BY DAVID KEMP

COLLECTED POEMS

BY

HENRY TREECE

1946 : ALFRED A. KNOPF : NEW YORK

821.91
T786c

ACKNOWLEDGMENTS

Acknowledgments are due to the periodicals and anthologies listed below, which have printed poems included in the present volume:

Accent, The Adelphi, Compass, Dint, Diogenes, The Dublin Magazine, Fantasy, Furioso, Here and Now, Horizon, Kingdom Come, La France Libre, Life and Letters Today, The Listener, The New English Weekly, The New Republic, Opus, Poetry (Chicago), *Poetry* (London), *Poetry* (Scotland), *Poetry Folios, Poetry Quarterly, The Poetry World, Providence Sunday Journal, Seven, Time and Tide, The Tramp, Tribune, View, The Virginia Spectator, Voice of Scotland, Voices, Wales; Air Force Poetry* (John Lane, the Bodley Head), *The Best Poems of 1943, Bugle Blast* (Allen & Unwin), *A Celtic Anthology, The Crown and Sickle, The Exiles' Anthology, Little Reviews Anthology, Modern Reading, Modern Welsh Poetry* (Faber), *More Poems from the Forces* (Routledge), *The New Apocalypse, New Poems 1944* (Howell, Soskin), *New Roads 1943* (Grey Walls Press), *Poems to France* (La France Libre), *Poetry in Wartime* (Faber), *Transformation* (Gollancz), *View Poets, Wartime Harvest, The White Horseman, Writing Today* (Staples); and to *The Favil Press, The Runa Press, James Decker,* and the *British Broadcasting Corporation,* which has broadcast several of the poems.

H. T.

PUBLISHER'S NOTE

This book contains all of the poems that originally appeared in
Invitation and Warning (London: Faber & Faber; 1942), and
The Black Seasons (London: Faber & Faber; 1945), as well as
most of those in *38 Poems* (London; The Fortune Press; n. d.),
and many later, hitherto unpublished poems.

CONTENTS

Mystic Numbers
Pilgrim 3
Welsh Choir 3
The Dyke-Builder 4
Old Welsh Song 4
Poem ("Oh, God, your blood . . .") 5
Poem ("Oh, little child . . .") 5
What Thing Affrights You . . . 6
Through the Dark Valley . . . 6
The Three Houses 7
The House of Truth 8
Invitation and Warning 8
Three Ages 9
Poem ("I dropped the crock . . .") 9
Tale 10
Poem ("I made a cloak of music . . .") 10
The Characters 11
Song 11
Ballet 12
The Two Souls 12
Poem ("End and beginning . . .") 13
Pastoral 13
City 14
The Ghosts 14

The Warrior Bards 15
Horror 16
Rustic Charm 16
Dramatic Interlude 17
The Lying Word 17
How Sweet Are the Flutes! 18
Pastoral 1941 19
Ballad of the Ranting Lad 19
Homage to A.E.H. 20
Venus from the Waves 21
Elegy Unending 21
Poem ("What song is sweet . . .") 23
Wedding Song 23
Confession in War-Time 24
Legend 25
Inscription on a Begging Bowl 25
The House 26
The Never-Ending Rosary — A Sequence 27
Towards a Personal Armageddon — A Sequence 40
The Boat Returns 53
Poems from a Work in Progress 59
Death Mask 69
See-Saw on Dying 70
The Seasons 70

ix

Emperor Zero on Death	71	There is a Cause for	
The Homeless	72	Faith	102
Poem for Easter	73	The Varied Faces	103
Psalm Carved from		Christ Child	103
Sorrow	74	Betrayal	104
The Poet	75	Second Coming	
"I Locked Love's Door"	75	*Resurrection*	105
In Such a Wilderness		*The New Way*	105
as This	76	*The Seasonal Mind*	106
Remembering Last Year	77	*The Sermon in the*	
Poem for Christmas	77	*Field*	107
The Three Selves	78	*Second Crucifixion*	108
Winter 1939	78	*A Thief to his Lord*	108
The Old Ones	80	*A Young Nun to her*	
Age	80	*Lover*	109
The Black Book	81	Love Poem	110
Sonnet	82	Love Song	110
Relics	83	Tears Are Too Small	111
Birdwatcher	83	Oh Child	111
The Magic Wood	84	Dumb Love	112
The Crimson Cherrytree	86	Revenante	112
The Lost Ones	87	Captured Moment	113
Boat Blessing	92	The Dilemmas	113
Bard's Lament	93	Love Sonnet	114
Blind Bard	93	Ophelia	114
The Heroes	94	Sad Song	115
Evacuation from the		The Ballad of the Prince	
Isles	97	*Prologue*	116
The Shadows of My		*The Ballad of the*	
Words	98	*Prince*	117
Fugitive	98	*His Coming and the*	
The Possessors	99	*Fear*	117
Poem	100	*The Wizard's Daugh-*	
Varied Growing	100	*ter*	119
Three Steps for a Poet	101	*The Prince Passes*	123
The Barriers	102	*A Courtier Speaks*	125

The Shepherd Lad's Lament	126	Birds	147
		Circle	148
Epilogue	128	Poem ("The word that lies inside the head . . .")	148
Ballad	129		
War Poem	130		
To Certain Ladies on Going to the Wars	131	Sympathy with Stone	149
Prayer in Time of War	132	Poem ("Who murdered the minutes . . .")	149
Poem Before the End	132		
The Conscripts	133	Poem ("Call me the Twelve . . .")	150
Conqueror	134		
Martyr	136	Poem ("When quiet comes . . .")	151
To the Edge and Back	136		
Lyric	144	The Lantern and the Ghost	151
Lincolnshire Bomber Station	144	Poem ("Blood in the bud . . .")	152
The Heart's Wild Geese	145	Y Ddraig Goch	153
Walking at Night	146	Plaint	154
In the Third Year of War	146	Victor and Vanquished	154
Three Pleas	147		

COLLECTED POEMS

MYSTIC NUMBERS

I
PILGRIM

I step from a land no eye has seen
To a land no hand may ever hold;
My name with the sea's cold tears is green,
My words are the wind's words graved in gold.

This scrip upon my back holds hearts
That saw their hero in a dream;
This staff is ward against the darts
That stiffen trout in silver stream.

So, pilgrim, continents I tread,
The cross-bones in my breast for rood,
Breaking the shepherd's dusty bread,
The brittle beech leaves in the wood.

II
WELSH CHOIR

A bird sang to me out of Wales;
But, O man, the blood and the tears!
And the wild wild wailing in the hills,
And Caradoc's gore aflame on the moors.

3

A man spoke to me out of Wales
And the thin thin wind was in his voice;
Black thunder rolled in the bellowing vowels
And brought a drowned kingdom to my eyes.

Ten children sang to me out of Wales,
And the blood and the tears and the wind were there.
But the bright bird whistled: 'These little girls
Know the words, not the agony. They were not there!'

III
THE DYKE-BUILDER

On the seventh day the storm lay dead.
The god who built the dyke strolled out to see
Blind men, blind windows, widows and the daft,
And the cracked shore carpeted with gulls.

On the ninth day no sunset red
Daubed the damp stubble: peacock-blue, bright harmony
Of gold and purple laced the sky, and soft,
Ripe as a plum with joy danced the quick girls.

But on the eleventh day the dead
Looked from their priest-holes, seeing only sea,
And the green shark-cradles with their swift
Cruel fingers setting the ocean's curls.

IV
OLD WELSH SONG

I take with me where I go
A pen and a golden bowl;
Poet and beggar step in my shoes,
Or a prince in a purple shawl.

4

I bring with me when I return
To the house that my father's hands made,
A crooning bird on a crystal bough,
And O, a sad sad word!

V

POEM

Oh, God, your blood swings in my heart,
Your breath sweeps through my breast;
My love flames upward like a torch,
Link-bearer to your feast.

Oh, man, your word rides on my tongue
To praise this lovely land —
But must my shade lie cruciform,
This thorn pierce my thin hand?

VI

POEM

Oh, little child, see how the flower
You plucked bleeds on the iron ground;
Bend down, your ears may catch its voice,
A passionless low sobbing sound.

Oh, man, put up your sword and see
The brother that you did to death;
These is no hatred in his eye,
No curses crackle in his breath.

5

Walk through the world, you men, with me
As far as faith's far parish bounds;
Oh, brothers, fear not these great beasts,
Who are but God's own testing-hounds.

VII
WHAT THING AFFRIGHTS YOU . . .

What thing affrights you, lovely ghosts,
And why those staring eyes?
Is it a terror I may know
That starts those rending sighs?

'Young man, young man, we know your face,
We know the touch of your hand.'
What is it, brother, that brings you pain,
I'll crush it with that hand.

'It is no horror with heart for your prayer
Nor beast with blood for your sword.'
What is it comrade, my soul is yours?
'It is your own dark word.'

VIII
THROUGH THE DARK VALLEY . . .

Through the dark valley that I tread
In my hempen robe with staff for sword,
I see death's buds on every bough,
And smell decay in the raven's word.

Beneath each stone I know old lips
Are waiting to mock as I make my way;
Each stream will spawn a thousand snakes
To fondle my thighs as I kneel to pray.

But one thing keeps my head from harm,
Though cross upon my breast should flame,
Or knife should cut me to the heart —
The simple knowledge of a name.

IX
THE THREE HOUSES

Three flowers I tend in the house of faith,
The white, the gold and the red;
Speaking the spell through a silver horn
That shall bring a princess to my bed.

In death's grim house I act a prayer,
From the red-rimmed chalice drain a toast
To the white-lipped guardians I hear in the air,
And my father's gentle ghost.

In the house of love I name a name,
The candle starts to hear my voice.
But it's not with fear that my heart leaps when
I lift the latch and meet her eyes.

X
THE HOUSE OF TRUTH

Love has no limits like the year,
Nor like the word depends on breath;
Desire is started by a tear,
And Passion dances after Death.

All, all is truth for who dare seek,
And seeking, never fear to find;
From dreams a splendid house they make
Build solid on the shifting wind.

The knife that purifies the heart
Leaves soldier bleaching in the sand;
And rains that rot the future's bread
Make sweet the gardens of the mind.

XI
INVITATION AND WARNING

Pluck my fruit, the pear-tree said.
As you travel down the river.
Stay and sleep in my green hair.
The weed said to the drover.

Watch for snake and poisoned dart
As you cross the mountain;
Guard against the broken heart
As you pass the fountain.

Fruit will feed and weed will soothe,
But snake will sting and dart will pierce,
Vaulting hailstones crack the bone,
And hearts will give themselves to none.

8

XII
THREE AGES

My dream's steel mirror in this aspen-hand
Brings me the bare grey steppes of understanding,
Where on the oceanic hills of yesterday
A corpse of hallowed sticks rocks in the wind.

To-day's young creature yet aflame with love
Strides through life's nettles with a wand of gold,
Crops the foul fruits of evil, in the devil's teeth,
Smiling, knows not the world he soon shall leave.

But the uncoffined lad who waits the dawn
No prickle plucks, nor craves no silken sin,
Sits silent, watching the frail father's hand
Steal softly towards the poisoned drinking horn.

XIII
POEM

I dropped the crock of my love across the years,
Over the hills of joy, the woods of woe,
Over the sibilant seas that sang of death,
The deep unfathomed canyons of despair.

I spilled the oil of my wonder, spilled my tears,
Through the clouds of dismay: I watched them go,
Trailing like phantoms across the heath,
Where the three old men knelt, sad in prayer.

And I came at the end of the road of my life
To a hill and a throng and a man on a tree,
And I saw the gold boy I had got in my dream
Rise and come forward, with faith in his eyes.

9

XIV
TALE

There was a tale told on a winter's night,
Deep in the forest where never soul dared,
How the hanging man from the tree came down
And skipped in a polka with an old goat-herd.

And they say, they say, as the crisp logs crack,
'When Jack Frost comes, the ground is hard
For poor bare feet, and the wind too sharp
To dance in the woods with a wounded side.'

XV
POEM

I made a cloak of music from my dreams,
Gilt-thread for joy, and jet for years of sin,
Broidered the edges with the lace of love,
Softened to grey with tears no eye could hold.

And with this cloak about me, over streams
That led to Heaven's hills, I ran,
Crying aloud my father's name. His dove
Dropped from the boughs of Paradise. Unfurled,

The wings of wisdom warned me; many times
Harsh blows upon my heart bade me begone.
Yet thrust I sunward, till at close of eve,
I saw my father — nailed across the world.

10

XVI
THE CHARACTERS

The man in the mask swings a sword of bright stars,
The cloud of his breath is the shroud of the earth.
But the man in the robe from a book reads our fears,
And ticks off the minutes from death until birth.

The woman in white is the mother of hope,
And the twin doves of peace rest on her twin breasts.
But the woman in black, with a knife and a rope,
Is the watcher at gateway, the guardian of ghosts.

XVII
SONG

The song that the old woman sings in the lane
Is the song of the girl with the golden hair,
Of the gaunt old man who danced in the rain,
And the soldiers who ran from his eyes in fear.

And the song skips on, how the lass and the man
Lived in the woods with roots for their meat:
Friendly to fox, they laughed as they ran
Over the hills, the stars their loot.

But the tale ends, how in the full of their pride
The goose-girl woke from her tinkling dreams,
To find the man dead with a sword in his side,
And his beautiful brow gashed with three sharp thorns.

XVIII
BALLET

In a world of black velvet
The pale figure leaps
With a lath in his hand, while trumpet
With icicle-fingers slips
The bolts of the heart and enters the room,
Proving to man that life is a dream
And the man and the lath are things of the world,
That the black velvet stays when the tale has been told.

In a shroud of white cotton
The pale figure lies
With a bead in her hand. The beaten
Earth tingles with feet of the wise
Who this day have sung for a soul that has fled
To the mansion they builded to house the wise dead.
But men without wisdom are muttering now:
'Which trumpet will warn us, and where shall we go?'

XIX
THE TWO SOULS

The widowed soul sat staring through her hands,
Robed in no raiment but despair's thin shroud,
Garbed in no garment but mad grief's green shade,
And the apples of her love lying rotten on the ground,
And the long green-grief song moaning round the home.

The solitary soul no mate had ever met,
Walked in the talking shadow of the wood,
Heard with her wise virginity the voice
Of children from the barren bough of plum,
And felt the brittle twig snap pointed in her side.

XX
Poem

End and beginning are two wise words,
Two ways the wind blows in one breath;
Coming and going are movements both
That swing the door and bend the boards.

Four hands show weakness, stumble tongues;
Both heads are bare, the eyes are dim.
'Oh, the life of things is a difficult dream':
Two puzzled hearts croon fearful song.

Starting and finishing are two known ways
Of moving and halting, waking from sleep
To the land where blind watch lame men leap:
Two ways the leaf wags in the trees.

XXI
Pastoral

I have learnt nothing from the marble urn
That sparrow could not teach me. Overhead,
The same cloud loiters that has loitered through
A thousand poets' summer dreams.

'I have seen nothing new,' says marble urn,
'Since I was made. Alas, the many dead
Are more, but that is all. Above, below,
The same clouds, the same streams.'

XXII
CITY

Abrupt, unfluid as an eagle's love,
Stone's frozen tumult rears itself from fields,
Housing from germ to worm the flower of faith,
The pock-patched beggar and the marble saint.

Here, Christ and Judas walk upon the stream,
The strict stone river, in their hosts;
Hard as a pauper's prayer, the stone tree shades
From tempest the unprofitable birds.

Here, the stern moment hides above the cloud,
Strange music shocks the hand of carven men
Who knew no symphony but song of stone:
'How will destruction fall,' they beg, 'how death?'

But, shut from terror and the toppling plinth,
Drugged with the dream of plover's scream on hills,
Two lovers stand, and from reaction's hand
Scatter humanity across the park.

XXIII
THE GHOSTS

Through the plumed valley of despair come riding ghosts,
Their dripping lanterns swinging down my dreams,
Guests of the broken heaven in my heart,
Draping with dog-rose coffins that I carved
For other heroes than my dram-slain self.

14

Out of my breast breaks penance, like a sigh
Lost in a silent room of dust, where dead
Hands are clasped in memory, and clock
Only in vision knows again the voice
That spoke a music over half the world.

But dreams and deeds, head, heart, and hands
Tenant a tower of brilliants that flash
Yet never burn. The dog before the gate
Digs pleasure from his hide, forgets to watch —
And so the ghosts ride howling to my door.

XXIV
THE WARRIOR BARDS

So they came riding
In red and in gold,
With laughter and harping,
Over the wold.

No sword was among them,
They fought with a song,
Safe in their kingdom,
The children of Spring.

Only their falcons
That watched from above
Knew the grey tokens
And heard the black hoof.

And so broke the battle.
I watched their gay dead
Ride the gaunt cattle
Back through the wood.

XXV
HORROR

Like the fey goose-girl in the enchanted wood,
Whose cloth-of-gold hair curtained her swart sin
So that the feckless linnets stricken by her flute
For homage' sake forgot the bodkin bright,
And so lay waxen in among the moss
About her feet.

Like the gold boy, the weeping pauper prince
Prisoned in a tower of tongues and eyes,
Stumbling from floor to dusty screaming floor,
Upstairs and down stone stairs, whose flaking edge
Is brown with brother's blood. And brother's song
Shrill in his ears.

Like the old traveller, who knew this stormy road
Even before the raven sowed its elms,
Who comes by night upon a lighted house
Where no house was in any other year,
And stops, aghast, to see his own shade propped
Stiff at the board.

XXVI
RUSTIC CHARM

Wish in the well, at the lane's crooked limb,
Where the golden stoat his arabesque
Of evil weaves, with hare-paw charm:
That the sun-dappled apple tree fling her fruit
With the crystal-crash of the catkin-bomb,
And that where they fall five maids unmask
The hurrying heart that keeps them warm,
And five thin shifts slip to their feet.

16

XXVII

DRAMATIC INTERLUDE

But more than the death of a dream, the prince now stark in a sty,
And the hunters after truffles tearing the parquet floor;
More than that, the red lips raped by the shepherd's bread
And the banners scaring away the crows; yes, more than all,
Is the sad stone room and the worm-pocked board, the spider's
    husk
Tinkling as truant winds play hide-and-seek in rafters;
And the wild old man (his wife laid-out in the house in the wood)
Scratching the walls for gold, his dusty bread forgot,
Ransom for scriptural shades that glare from the ash
Of his grey fire, muttering alone, bidding arise
And walk again in beauty his pale mate. None
Hears him, knows him, but the rat hid in the thatch.

XXVIII

THE LYING WORD

Truth and lie by lip and tooth
Chase the face of every world;
Proud behind the probing eye
Is dream that throat throws out as word.
The ghost that jumps from dancing jaws,
Festive as creature crouched in a flower,
Pricks his tracks in plastic time,
For a future that fails with the falling hour.

Present and past pace in a vowel,
A consonant brings birth or death;
From womb to tomb is a letter's length
Where Capricorn can belt the earth.

17

Mouth's cavern mothers a brood of bright rats;
An alphabet of peace the tongue
Shapes to a shuddering treachery,
A carol with a death-bell clang.

The dead who died but yesterday,
The dead who yet dare to be born,
Know, and shall know this golden sword
That swings from the stump of the healing thorn.
But who can save us, who shall master
This mumming mould behind the mask?
The foetal fact that a gesture gags?
O what is this wind-shape word, this husk?

XXIX

How Sweet are the Flutes!

How sweet are the flutes, whose mellow notes
Travel together through flower-flecked fields,
Husband and wife; Question and Answer
Harnessed in harmony, waking old worlds.

Swift snakes of sound, fresh with desire,
They slide through the thickets Time has let slay
The proud palace garden that clamoured with colour,
To strike the low windows blind in bright day.

They pierce the high hedges, writhe over walls,
To the room where the lady waits, white with love;
They redden her lips and put pearls in her hair,
And leave the heart fluttering quick as a dove.

O sweet are the flutes! Their maddening notes
Tie with silk melody's noose the hands,
Keep shackled the sword and stabled the steed,
And leave men in mocking, impossible lands!

XXX
PASTORAL 1941

From bread and wine and the holy sticks
Now comes no peace.
High in the wind the bound bell rocks;
Should binding break, the brazen voice
Yell horror through the hand-sized cottage panes,
And herdsman finger bayonet in the lanes.

The walnut gipsy high on the downs
Stifles his fire,
Stills children's voices as the groans
Of dying cities plead in his ear.
There are no seasons now for pipe and drum;
The steel birds never migrate from our dreams.

XXXI
BALLAD OF THE RANTING LAD

He built him a home, the rapscallion lad,
In a turned-up boat on a lonely shore,
And peopled it with a prince's dream,
Was happy in rags if the fire burned clear.

He took him a wife, this bright-eyed boy,
With snowy breast and golden hair,
And they laughed the length of a summer's day
If pear-tree bore and the fish leaped fair.

He got him a boy, young devil-may-care,
To talk to and dangle upon his knee,
And gave him a name and a cloak of wool,
And gospels heard in the words he would say.

19

Then wild waves broke and broke the home,
And fever came for the golden child.
When grey dawn knocked, in her workhouse shift,
The girl lay stiff as a stone with cold.

But the rollicking boy, the rapscallion lad,
Took up his stick, made a fool of his pain,
And walked on the hills with a dream in his sack,
Of a house and a wife and a twittering bairn.

XXXII
HOMAGE TO A.E.H.

Oh, sigh no more, my lady,
Sweet Spring must come again
To glad the hedge with violet
And bless the bud with rain.

Oh, weep no more, my poppet,
Though hell fall from the skies;
You'll want those golden tresses,
He'll need those sparkling eyes.

For many a man there'll be still,
Oh, many a lusty lad.
Don't let them go a-begging
For what they never had.

The lark must sing his song, love,
If from a splintered wood;
And bayonet's edge grow rusted,
Though rusted in my blood.

So sigh no more, my lady,
Sweet sleep shall come again
To kiss you in your bed, lass,
With some peace-lucky man.

XXXIII
VENUS FROM THE WAVES

See the dying girl float
In her bed's pale shell.
Stripped of its flowers, her boat
Swings on the intermittent swell.

The weeping world stops
In its plaintive sombre song,
Its tears are crystal drops
Shed for a love gone wrong.

The girl in a vision meets
Love drowned in green furrows, dead . . .
In the foam of the ruffled sheets
Her long hair floats like weed.

From Federico García Lorca.

XXXIV
ELEGY UNENDING

A rose is in the hand,
A tear is in the eye;
You will never understand
Why I must cry.

A wind disturbs the water
And bends the back of tree;
In wind there is a laughter.
But not in me.

My eyes tell me a house
Is empty now and bare;
My ears say not a mouse
Can forage there.

My fingers tell a stone
That bears a graven name;
Oh, body that is bone
Is not the same!

In sleep I hear a song
Whose words I knew before.
They sing it still, along
The tidal shore.

By day I smell the scent
Of Austria's lilac-tree;
I feel its balm is lent
By her to me.

And a rose is in the hand,
A tear is in the eye;
But you'll never understand
Why I must cry.

XXXV
POEM

What song is sweet
Beside the touch of hand upon the head?
What marble goddess
Half so fair as wife beside my bed?

What word is strong
Beside the thrust of flower through the soil?
What worth the mail
That's set against the isolated soul?

I have known death
March in the mind of smiling-gestured saint;
I have seen love
Choose for his home the harlot-ridden haunt.

Shall song and sword,
Saint, drab and death, draw patterns in the air,
To die straightway;
Or shall their warning flare like forest fire?

XXXVI
WEDDING SONG

You shall have roses, my sweet,
And a lantern to frighten the owl,
And a nutmeg tree in the garden,
And pears in a golden bowl.

And I will buy you a bird
With feathers bright as blood,
And a door with lock and key
For our lonely house in the wood.

23

XXXVII
CONFESSION IN WAR-TIME

Once, long ago, I ran beneath the sun,
Loved his warm hand upon me, kind as fur;
With arms and legs I swung a wide world over,
Brother to men of ice and girls of fire.
Then, words were air, and only hands showed hearts,
And only hearts showed love, or only hate;
Between the two worlds tinkling in my head
There was no place for poetry, no seat
Where I as white-haired shadow of myself
Could sit and count the hours, call to the feet
Of lusty bone and blood that bore my soul
Each minute nearer to perdition's gate.

Now, not so much older, yet so old,
The fire is smothered, and my roaring men
Have whisked away my maidens to a land
Where they can laugh beneath another sun.
This hand, poor prince, that swung a rascal's stave,
Now prideless, begs a favour from the pen;
These eyes, now dull, that once a god's world knew,
Will glitter only in that moment when
They see I still exist upon a page.
My two worlds gone, I tread now like a ghost,
Intangible and featureless, alive
Only as letters crossing in the post.

XXXVIII
Legend

There was a man
With a coloured coat of rags
Who left his body and blood on a tree.
But the thieves at his side gave the bones to the dogs,
And the black-thorn cock sang merrily.

The lads of the town
Drank down to the dregs
Then took a sharp axe to lop the tree.
But the thieves had been there first gathering logs,
And the black-thorn cock sang steadily.

One day at dawn
Upon their nags
Twelve tinkers came and their hearts were free,
For they cut twelve whistles from the knuckles of the dogs,
To bear the black cock company.

XXXIX
Inscription on a Begging Bowl

The way the cloak falls
Is majesty;
The way an eye falls
Is modesty;
The way a bird falls
Is destiny;
The way a coin falls
Is charity.

How then when the cloak is flaunted by leper,
And hidden eye is the eye of a whore?
How then when the hawk shall fall for a feather,
Coin pay the reckoning for bloody war?

XL
THE HOUSE

The hollow shell of a house
Is not the body and blood;
The brain, the fire and the flesh
Live not in bones of wood.

The soul is never seen,
Intangible as air;
It is the love of the man
Whose children live there.

THE NEVER-ENDING ROSARY—
A SEQUENCE

INTRODUCTION

I dig this sonnet from a soil of years
Manured by mournful minutes, wet by the rain
Of carefree summers spent by God's salt seas.
The pale boy staring through the dusty pane,
Small finger tracing future on the glass,
Is my small ghost; the very lad who strode
The yawning plains of Europe, round whose fires
Poet and beggar broke a dreamer's bread,
Spinning such webs of magic that their words
Sped in the tree-tops, joyful as quick jays,
Made Christ a comrade, tender of the herds
Out on wind's acre, one of the roaring boys;
And Hamlet, silent at the wood's edge by my side,
Another lad with grey hairs in his head.

I

Slow sarabande of pain in all the air;
Everywhere cadence, decay of a tune, of time,
Death of the gold days and the feathered joy,
And across the purple hills and the purple sky
The long undying rosary of despair.

It has come too soon, this sorrow's psalm,
The dog-faced cloud-rack scowling in the West,
Where brethren moving like uprooted trees
In a Birnam of blood drop aching twigs of hands,
And from leaves in an ancient way stare round about

At callous undulating plains of salt,
Where nightjar leers through a broken note,
And the scarecrow dog at the end of his rope
Gnaws at the door, howls as he feels as we,
The wide immeasurable knowledge of an end.

II

Sharper than ever, the bright beaks of words
Charm my slim finger. In a full-table time
Even the sockets of my head sprout words
That scream and whimper through my dreams like birds
Lost in a desert, or, as the mandrake calls,
A purple rhetoric among the midnight stones.

As flood upon the drum inside my head
Knocks with a ghostly hammer, so my heart,
Mistress of ice and heat, strings out a song
Of words and more than words, that baffle tongue,
And the red wine course after thought and thinker
Through lanes that bind my sword-hand to my sword.

In this winter it is the frozen word
That groans upon my doorstep; as Spring buds,
The word whose nest of gold hangs in the sticks;
The tale that kindles in the hyacinth,
Sweeter than civet in a lady's bower, is word,
And word that wrinkles as the red leaf falls.

The bones of words long dead ride on the wind
That sweeps my searching eyes along the years
From blackness into blackness, till like the bird
Our fathers guessed, the word of truth, in light
Stands bare for one brief footfall — then is gone,
And wind blows where he listeth through the tombs.

III

From that hard minute when the tortured womb
Dropped me, the wailer, in a stone-faced world,
My double-crossing soul has worn two masks;
One hides the singer, his shy foot in the tomb,

While summer poems to the stars he whirls;
One, the hard-headed, keeper of the home,
Hater of blue-eyed darling and the frilled
Fancies of the boy who takes no risks.

'Love and let thrive,' says one, 'the bearded word
Wait on the marring morrow for its answer;
Let me sing softly,' says this lad of love,
'Stroking the minutes, precious in my palm,
Winding my wishes round me when the wind's hard.
I'll move from danger like a supple dancer,
My feet familiar with the flowers they cleave,
And in the coloured caverns build my home.'

'What whirlpool's in the skull that with my hand
I dare not halt? What passion could not purge?
I tower above the pigmy centuries,
Blow the years down and chuckle at their crash,'
Says other, laughing through the tired land.
'What songs might I declaim for horny age,
Who know not size of pain, or where fear is?
Duty alone is death and foreign to my wish.'

Which shall be mine, worn as my daily face,
When penny's itch and duty's pen have etched
Their laws upon me? Which my safe epitaph?
Will either swing a sword and dry my fears?
Bosom, hold both! that both the boys I hatched
Bend a blind ear to Satan as he roars;
So shall my devil from his rock be dashed,
Death fall face downwards, riddled by one truth.

IV

What coiner carved his mark upon my heart
Before the womb forsook me, flung me to fate?
These hands that feel the future, whose are they?

Some monster strung my veins in lover's knot
And wrapped my eyes with words his father wrought
But never taught me. Whose this mad mummery?

'Who is this mocker, my maker,' I ask, 'my friend?'
Not God, whose bread explodes inside my mouth?
Pied-piper madness this benefactor loves,
Whose words of peace ignite within my hand
As I offer his leaden pence for food; his truth
Fickle as breeze-twitched boughs about the eaves;

Not Time that paints his dearth upon the bough,
For death upon the rose is my death too,
Rings my heart's bells and drinks my babbling blood,
And over the salt seas blows my frail fever. Though
Tongueless, my fingers' voice attack this foe
The nagging winds, his henchmen, waste my word.

When Death has pressed his image in my face
There can be no more doubt, no more despair;
And love and loss, soft in a bed together,
Talk me a dirge meet for my fruitless age,
Laugh at my corpse, who on its broken bier
Wide-eyed with terror waits this forgotten father.

V

The will that keeps me fettered in the world
Is not my own. Mine is no lackey-love
For spindle-shanks, and, listening to the old,
I save my breath to snigger up my sleeve
At Sunday-face with bibles in his voice
Who, gospel-gargling, treads upon the rose.

A candle shows me where the sword has bred
The lightless eye, the dead bird on the bough,
And ravening counties eating flesh for bread:

Lift up those boards and you will find below
A bullet-riddled prayer-book on whose leaves
Another decade's rats have writ their loves!

World's womb, unchilded, shelters in its rooms
A treeless country and a crippled god,
And southern suns, never more near than dreams,
Slide like a tipsy wench across the globe.
I could have saved them, but they burnt my heart,
And wrapped their ears with riddles while I roared.

God, that the mole should dig and threadbare wolves
Howl round the vineyards at a hungrier foe!
What is the reason that the rain should fail,
That fruit should fall, and fish rot in the sea?
To me it is divine incompetence
That shall go loveless if we love our sons.

VI

I have seen Winter's pale hand halt on the bud
With the charm of a saint, and a serpent's wile,
And the cow-patched path a-swarm with folk
Whose garnished caps in festival
Flew between eyes and the broken byre
And the dank straw mouldering from the roof.

I have watched, as I walked, in the boy's hard hand
The fractured bird, the fruitless egg:
In the innocent eye, the oaken step,
And the dewdrop diamonds in his hair,
Heart has discerned the disease of youth,
Wild screams from the stairs in a lonely house.

These things are known as a knot is tied,
As a pitcher breaks they are forgot;
So the merry huntsman, red in the woods,

31

Draws not his rein as the hare's heart breaks,
But rides with a song to his father's gate,
There to be gay with death's next guest.

VII

I have known Winter in a time of tears
Walk through the land with burning eyes
To lay men low. In Spring, on rack of words,
Gold hearts have twisted, all because a wind
Has with a ruffian-hand bid blood be high,
And swing his bully shoulders in a crowd.

I have known Summer tell another tale
Than Summer in the song and dance has told;
How in the fields, under a feathered sky,
Young hand has slackened and the eye seen shapes
That haunt the mother-season in a land
Sick to the heart with words, with words of brass.

Only in Autumn, only before the knock
Of bone upon the sheltering oak is heard,
Shall the still peace of suffering be known:
Only in Autumn, when rash blood be let
And garden-spirals show the end of lust,
Smiles tired heart and hearthside words fly free.

VIII

When Spring's caress and when the winds of love
Undo the dog that whines within my blood
And canker in my heart withdraws his siege,
Masters, my hands hew patterns in the airs,
Weave pick-lock magic, open up the grave!
Power more than Moses struck for rocks my head,
Masking my mewler with a wizard face
Whose maledictions flicker, bright as stars.

What body's sin has severed I can knit
In that mad moment: what the heart desires
These hands can hold, hold healing of the pain
That rocks a monarch on his painted throne.
These feeble hands set fallen mountains up,
This little finger flicks out forest fires.
I am the man my father envied men,
Whose lucky soul lives lecherous as the wren!

What man has done and lived to tell the world
I'll do again. I'll dare the dragon's wrath,
And in the company of angels bawl the word
That baffles oracles, makes dead bones ring,
And palm the celestial ace in Jahweh's fold.
Or let the tiger-smiling, suave boy of truth,
Track my heart down, my wanderer in the wood,
Twitch the bent stick and put an end to song.

Yet time shall be, noiseless as sea-shell sounds,
When death shall knock me cold and my last word
Wail like a little ghost about the parks;
When tiny shapes with flowers in their eyes
And sick-room voices, weeping from their wounds,
Move slow as centuries about my bed.
Then what my gain, if scorpion-terrors lurk
To tear my Hamlet-heart out on the rose?

IX

Between the female sticks I tasted hell
Garnished with flowers: under its mask the skull
Mocked my poor flesh's labour, foisted the lilt
Of lust upon me, led me a dance and laughed
At body's fever. Dour death in bone
Bent my frail twig, turned song to stone.

33

The King, my father, wrought me sunlight songs,
Meet for the golden board, the blood-red wine:
The Queen, men's mistress, mastered me in wrongs,
Then plucked my eyes to feed her noble swine,
Shot me the hawk who took my message,
Left me a cell, a dungeon dotage:

Built in a breath, the magic of the morning,
Killed at a glance, the beauty of the night:
(Nothing is sacred when I tell its story,
And flowers rot where flowers grew in my heart)
Call high, call low, the ghost you'll find
The day you can surprise the wind.

Heart-high the callow hangman swings my fears,
The scarecrow deeds that shudder in the light,
He knows my price (a ducat buys my tears),
He knows my fate — love in the dog-days bought,
Holds me for less than gutter-nurtured creature
Who does deny his blood, his very nature.

And who denies him? Darnel, dock and rue
The only chorus when he runs me through.
(Heaven's outcast, clasping the dark ducat in his claw!
The twisted emblem of age is in me now!)
Let the play follow, the arrased rat play high,
If it go well, then I will name a comedy!

X

After a little while all grief lies dead,
And hands and madness in the eyes are still;
Worn heart awakes to find all tears are shed,
To shout a new song as feet climb other hill.
So they can rant, who can no longer feel,
Though Death with scissors nicks them like a fool.

I was the lad caught thunder in his cap,
And taught the hawk to carve his name on clouds,
Ragged the dumb oracle and drained the cup
Of sorrow for a wager; he whose needs
Were those alone that motivate the birds
To ride wild winds or rest content in woods.

But after faith and fame the gale blew round,
Back to its caverned home, and left him loose.
Then leaden words fell thud upon the ground,
Buying no tithe of truth, but only tears,
Bringing no candle to light him to his board
And bed, only Death's chopper to chop off his head:

Which had been there for him straight from pistol's crack
To croak of doom, from lilting cradle-rock
To the last strand of hemp that breaks his neck,
God's gift (whose presents must be given back)
To this soft dreamer, who, banquets in his soul,
Stumbles from Heaven with a ticket for the dole:

Whose words, like young unbedded virgins wail
About Love's temple, or in the midnight bed
Rap on his heart as blindly as the mole.
But they can knock till hand and heart are dead.
The corpse they crave is still as cold as stone,
And no flame flickers where there's only bone!

XI

This minute had been centuries on the way,
And centuries had ground my granite smooth;
Walls had grown high about my eyes, my ears,
But I had looked to love to fling these down.
Yes, the long years had nightly promised flowers,
Preached me a paradise, syrups in my mind.

But cloak hid sword and clock the swing of youth,
Flower sheltered adder, under stones a sting
Lurked, dreaming unwary feet: my feet, my heart,
Urchin though ancient, cozener, were fleeced;
And wind's voice, sack of orts, my centuries' dower,
Blown seed, was sea-thrown, rotten to the tongue.

The brittle world broke round me as I shrank,
Less-love and lack-pence, waiting for the blow;
Now ran the raping winter at my heels,
Promised before my cradle clutched its lord;
My making, my undoing, were not mine
But lay in the hands of angels, hands like claws.

So I lie shamed, discovered in a night
As dark as death, deeper than history;
Mocked from the flower's bell, scorned by the worm,
That pock-patched bitter brother whose is right
To shelter in my shroud, my final friend;
Thus taste I glory, friends, banquet on bones.

See-saw, my ticking heart will last to-day,
But the next and the next will be a reign of tears;
Some hill may own me once before the rats
Break through my box and forage for my hopes.
But hope has gone, and heaven's voice is thin;
Now only scarecrow deaf can know the dumb.

XII

If then a star should fall and singe my shroud
So that the gold-lipped legates of my god
Hold before horror fingers cruciform,
To purge the lilied pools where goddesses
And none but milk-white, sweet my pure-in-heart,
Had in delight bequeathed reflection:

If in my March-hare, turncoat breast
The elfin, festering barb of doubt should prick
Quick and cry halt! to fingers' templar-trade —
So should the promise slip from paradise,
Let lie along the lane my carrion hopes,
And the thin children of decay crouch in the hearth.

But, lest my lord should see me in such ruin,
Mountains should crumble, caverns pock the plains,
Strict columns rattle on the parchment fields
Like play-day drumsticks on a heaven of tin;
And like a looting angel's rod of fire,
Proud poplars prick the slow sun from the sky.

XIII

In heart's cracked bowl lie pence, that by my dream's
Slick counterfeit are coined, spun from the air
Like fabulous cloth-of-gold, prophet's cast clout
Upon the patient fool who waits below,
Spendthrift of molten minutes ere the Lord
Shall call him close to whisper in his ear;
The wastrel watcher of the weasel's craft,
Delicate instrument upon whose page will be
Forever stamped the poor daft coney's testament.

If at this bowl's rim flutes of other times
With salt-eyed melody and gilt despair
Make sharp assault, or red with ancient fire
The rage that burnt my fate upon my brow,
Crack the frail platter on whose side is scored
My history, shall faith fly out as fear?
Or may it be that, from the garden-croft
Another bright boy wrote of, blackbird's plea
Will soften even Satan's merriment?

Sometimes my finger, itching in the flames
Trull-tongue has kindled, knots for me a snare,
Or points me to the crowd like any liar;
Sometimes these eyes in riding high and low
Tease me with paradise as hawk plays bird.
Inner and outer tread the road to war,
And all Atlantis' sands left me to sift . . .
If laughter shake me from salvation's knee
Who shall be judge upon the harm I meant?

I only know the faggot of my flames
Is this same limb my father bade me bear;
This name that tumbles like a sodden lout
Out of the world's prim mouth shall come and go
Whatever weather fall, be frost so hard
That angler, patient at the future's weir,
Pluck it like feckless trout, stiff as a gift
Where given-to and giver smell the lie
That lurks unbidden underneath the scent.

XIV

Invention is the spirit's sharpest pain,
A midnight lamentation in the cell
Bled white with lack of saying. Quick as a fungus
In the crevice of the soul, stirs thought
That knows no word, no sunlight on the world,
And, like the silken-veinéd dove, about
The iron door of meaning breaks its pride.

Like rotting seas, with Moloch's harvest home
Writhing away to farthest journey of the eye,
Almost to end of limit-line of life,
The poems, that forever in my womb
Must suck their banquet only from my dreams,
Cry like a breastless babe in some strange house,
Forgotten, at the end of no-man's road.

So, think you not, when in a time of iron
My hand arises like a lilied saint
And begs the means from warder-world to carve
For future's dalliance, in a freckled stone,
These agonies of heart, sharp knives of tune —
So think you not assassin other hand
Which leaps like flame and plucks heart's twanging cord;

Which had been best done, as it was to be,
Before the sire had crept plague-blooded to
His purple palace of delight; before
Cell's curt invention to the winter light
Thrust out for all the grinning globe to see,
An alabaster angel, frail with truth,
Whose body be invention's battlefield.

XV

Slow sarabande of pain in all the air;
Everywhere cadence, decay of a tune, of time,
Death of the gold days and the feathered joy,
And across the purple sky and the purple hills
The long undying pattern of despair.

It has come too soon, this sorrow's psalm,
And the black cloud-rack scowling in the West,
Where brethren moving like uprooted trees
In a Birnam of blood drop aching twigs of hands,
And from leaves in an ancient way stare round about

At callous, undulating plains of salt,
Where nightjar leers through a broken note,
And the scarecrow dog at the end of his rope
Gnaws at the door, howls as he feels as we,
The wide, immeasurable knowledge of an end.

TOWARDS A PERSONAL ARMAGEDDON—
A SEQUENCE

I

The shapes of Truth are no man's history
Or hope; born in the horny womb of Time,
They die with the daylight, ere the Surgeon's hand
Can grasp the knife to solve the mystery
Of feeling and the half-formed word. Sand
Trickles slyly through the palm like this,
Playing the hour-glass with the living bone,
Wife to the midnight sigh, the foetal wish.

The tired poet in his reeling room
Twists thoughts to clothe his bare hypnotic words;
Distracted by the rain on sodden thatch,
He moves towards the window, lifts the latch,
Cries, crazed by some bloody incubus of doom,
'Oh, listen to the laughter of the birds!'

II

All life came to me in the bed of love.
I, blushing puppet, shaped in rose's mould,
Whose eyes rode southern airs, whose lips
Lisped the leaves' song and flailed the world with words.
From inch to acre is the eagles' vision,
Who clasp the tawny counties in a claw;
From now to ever is a hail of years,
Slow snail's the master and the stammering crows!
But in my passion lives of all I lived
And spoke their voices for a thousand years.
West-wind, my brother, took me by the hand
And showed me over hells my other homes;
So nightly, under sodden thatch I lay
And times before the tomb I heard my ends.

III

Before my tails began, before the light
Burst like a devil's howl behind my lids,
Words flickered in my skull and tied my tongue;
Twisting my garment's hem to gain a blessing,
Turning the words of love to gain a home,
I was the lad of sin whose heart bled tears.
Whose fickle pulse beat out all bodies' message?
And who but I had heard the weasel's woe?
Who told the tick of tide in petals' fall,
Knew how a world of years rides in a wind?
(That was a black beginning.) In my brain
The future's noisy crotchet scratched a niche,
Twisted my sombre soul in arabesque.
This was the fanfare to my fair-ground fate.

IV

Like a deft lecher, laughing in his hand,
Or flaming like gigantic stalactite,
I burst the web that kept me in the thighs,
Scattering my bloody pearls across the land.
Stars shook as my silver scream shore high
Into their hearts, and heaved a sigh that I
Should in that midnight minute shout
A song that other ears and other stars
Find but the birthing-ballad of a boy,
The baby-babble as the tooth breaks through.
From that dark minute I have felt my future
Stalk through the land and scythe the hours through,
While in the warm womb's cavern even,
I saw my hearse, felt the rough prick of shroud.

41

V

My tale of horror was the dry-drugged virgin,
The eyeless child with flowers in his claw.
My land of terror was the treeless country,
Whose warping womb held nothing but my fear,
Whose stone songs died before the mourning light.
These were my tale, my land, and these my tears.
If they had taught me ways and wiles of winds,
The fever of the cracked bone in the thigh,
I should have known the worst, and these dead days
Would not have dragged me like a dog to die,
Here in a land where no hand holds a greeting,
Where the slack jaw only the death-day mouths;
I could have known and could have swung my heart
To the place where lips labour alone with laughter.

VI

The wry world sucked me, gave me for a home
A leper's chancel; following the lion
I knew what banquets slept within a stone,
How that the cautious raven for his sins
Must pluck from lime-dry planets sustenance
And smile when gay-garbed adder milks the moon.
From this rock I chipped a short-life's grace
And flaked the minutes in my palm like rime,
Tasting them before they fell to dust.
Yet came the dawn when jackal-coat I sloughed
And, compound with treachery, I moved with snake;
Two-wise I stepped, deceiving as I dealt,
Learning to live on lies and love the pit;
Was this the start, or page before the end?

VII

Then slew I brother with a knife of words.
His body fell, and failing breathed the Spring.
Tree's hand and heart's side would have kept him warm,
But for the beggar in his blood that crowed,
Waking my pilgrim from his forest dream.
Alas, masters, who shall paint the corse
To make it feast-ways ready for my bride?
Who hold the chalice, lest the coursing stream
Should nourish ants who'd grow and rend my box,
Should teach the hawk my message through his tongue
And bring upon me terror as I slept?
The deed is dun: my hand's too weak for jet,
Justice would give me syrops for my brows,
Where others brandish thorn-crowns on a hill.

VIII

I took a man with eyes of pain, whose pearls
Pranking the rubble robbed me of my sleep:
I loved a man with a dagger of lath, lithe,
Lissom and lying, cut-purse with poet's tongue.
And these two-hearted chuckled at my ruin,
Crack-wit they called me, whispering to the trees.
But on the morrow, and the morrow's mother, I,
With gloves of silk and eagle's feathers fraught,
Crossed paths and sticks and let the black pool run
For one; for other, Jack the man of string
Did me a duty, then my fellow-trees
Braced bone and with their knotted muscle sank
A rope for dangling dalliers in the breeze.
Sap throve on bleeding, I on the living gold.

IX

Yet move they many, all their words are false,
And though their tongues swing sweetly southern airs,
The man they carve their image on is lost.
Stab one, swing one, drop one in the ditch,
Stitch ten for fishes in the miser's bag;
Rack one, crack one, bury deep in lime,
Yet rising sun shall see them, ten on ten,
Knocking the old note out of sea-shore shells,
Cozening the old man ready for the hearse,
Alive, loved and moving, many in their lies,
While I, time-master, lord of gallow-tree,
Shall watch them speechless, dancing as they go,
Shaking the rooftree, dropping blight on bough:
And mountains toppling from their velvet feet.

X

'Come night and come the sliding of the stars:
Come Angelus and sway the swinging teat,
That planets, suckled like a hungry stone
In henpecked heaven, scatter plaints abroad.
Colour me, lanterns, with a gibbet-dye
That tongue and eye out of my lantern skull
Shall chase the body-tasters from the globe,
And leave the mountain-summit free for love.'
This, in my mystic missal, wrote a saint,
Washing the sword and nail-prints in his side,
Watching the faded ages in his hair:
It was so long ago when I heard this;
The seeds I spat while walking in the fields
Now flourish figs and tempt my poacher-lips.

44

XI

A sack of weasels from the land of graves
Unwinds my wishes, strews abroad my hope.
And in the moonlight out upon the plains
A mole-dance stammers words from unboxed bones
That chill my ears and spike my habits through.
For peace I pack my eye, my altar change,
And sew nine stitches where was once a stake;
For love I lash flame nine-pins to my breast
And finger-way break minutes as they bud.
But it is useless: for along the lanes
The briar-claws clutch, the adder's nests lie low,
And it is only seconds till the sword
Shall nail me palmwards up against the oak.
(All which was writ me in a dream of rats.)

XII

There is a hill and over that a cross
Swung in a cloud, and over that a star.
There is a man, and over him a sword
Swung in a hand, and over that a god.
Who pays the piper if he is a demon?
Who calls the tune, if Michael rips it out
From gold-strings at heaven-gate when earth below is black
With ant-plague and penny itch and fever in the heart?
There is a mountain crawling as we sing,
Whose woods clothe giants' navels as we love.
And who shall bar the door against its day,
And who shall cut the bough and bow the churl?
Don't guess, don't labour for the word that's sped:
Don't lie awake, don't love, don't speak your name.

XIII

A dog coughs; who then shall doubt a wolf?
If clouds weep thistles, shall the bomber's egg
Bore, burrow its mole-hole in the coffin-wall?
Long have I watched the madness in my hand
And long felt terror chipping in my bone;
But I would hack this half-heart from its stalk,
Crush between mill-stones these my milksop struts
If finger's voice stroked mercy out of steel
Or visiting the hills I found I ran.
A wolf sings and who would smell a rat,
If ducat's devil had him, in the walls?
No, flags dance, and coloured altars rise
To praise the Spring that gives us ears to hear,
Hands to hold the weather, fledgling to feed.

XIV

A snake in thatch can spell the end of dreams,
Spill sun, the desert's cousin, out of doors
And drum the twitching hours from my wrist.
But snake in man spells not nor dreams a sun,
Spoils the bright flower and lets the red blood run,
Cozens the lock and knows all stars are free.
So of the two, the twin-legged and the none-,
Which shall we follow, festoon with our fears?
And which the one nail twisting to the barn
To brother weasel? Once in my life a dwarf
Lurched from an oak and rapiered a god,
Smiling, mouse-footed, with an arm of stone,
Then turned, curtsied to our smiles and tears,
Vanished between the rafters and the thatch.

XV

These many-storied pence will etch my dream
In pink-rock caverns underneath the moon;
Where, safe from the Age's rack, I'll spin a doom
For every stick that stabbed my wishes. Fame,
Fearful and frenzy-footed now my sable hand
Clasps hard and strangles earldoms in a trice,
Shall with a female gesture offer gold,
Toss with a downward glance the Indies' sack
And prayer of grasping. Yet I shall stand aloof,
Alone, building with words and winds a turret
Which my black book and block shall furnish quite;
Whose doors, deaf to the gold-edged pauper's paw,
Shall give no message of the man who waits,
Shall open suddenly without a sign.

XVI

For it was told me in a dream I heard,
When the ice-night blew windwise through my head
And taught my linnet-loves to rest in stones:
That night I saw an eagle twist a wheel,
Saw my own numbered name flash through a fire,
Heard my blood whisper that a time had trod
His passage round the stars and now had come;
Waiting, was tickling my heart-door with his scythe,
Counting his fretful hours till my hand knocked
Away the bolts to let him walk within.
So he stands here, grows old inside my veins.
Smaller than crags now, weaker than young lions,
His home became a place of hissing, leopard's fair,
I, masters, shelter, yet am his Master-grave!

XVII

The dancing man with the dagger of lath
Slashes the bubbles growing out of grief,
And drops the leaden hours through the loam.
He is the rainmaker, son of the fatal plight;
But the stumbling woman dressed in straw
Strews thorns, and scythes the merry moment's corn:
Her womb drops woe before her limbs have lived,
And her to-morrow died before the dawn.
Yet of the two, the lathman and the sheaf,
I'd give my ring where sorrow rings the clock.
We who are merely planets' tennis balls
Hold fast to tinsel, letting diamonds drop
Like damsel plums, into the poacher's hand,
And never read the world till we are blind.

XVIII

The bubble-word is nectar to the dumb,
And ghosts have wept at trifles over Thebes,
Where between sackcloth's lips and water's whip
Old men have spoke the deathbed of an Age.
Likewise the deaf have shuddered at the word
Wailed by a suckling scarcely dry from womb;
And scholars turned uneasy pages as
Crows croaking cross the silent pane.
What is the shape of truth? I ask. Are words
Coined in the catchpenny midnight, armour plate,
Bourn from the mourning moan, the morn
Of madness, when the roving eye feels rooms
And finds an empty house, his side-man stone?
Will words heal wounds that sharpen heartslike knives?

XIX

When yellow spots do on your hands appear
Think twice, thank God, but do not hope to act.
For midnight daggers rust in morning dew,
And sunlight on a wound will breed a fruit.
Wait, watch how the cypress dances for the moon,
The fluid geometry of bats, the black mole's trade,
And you will know how much a limb is worth,
How much St. Francis gathered in his cap:
And you will know what song the beetle sings,
And how the straw-built prophet comes to hell.
A white horse proudly walked along a hill,
Bearing an eagle, who with bloody claw,
Tore out its entrails just before the wall;
I saw the horse blaze banners from his eye.

XX

'Tis not the painted stick, the golden boy,
The figure cut in alabaster pays
Me for the bearing burden of a name:
These baubles sat my eyes like shiftless wench,
Heated my loin, but left it cold as stone,
And no love lost, and no love to be gained.
Twelve-tongued the Bell Hosannah paints a grave,
One-piped the devil-kestrel Eden wings:
And I am here in matter without mould,
Manwise to walk where walking brings no home,
Where homes can hold no hearts a moment's space,
Where walls hold mirrors which alone hold walls.
If there's a hill worth climbing, tell me, boy,
What's on the other side, mountains or plains?

XXI

What hand of stone has stabbed my hope,
And writ my fate upon a talking dial?
Was it the same forking limb that hacked a cross
Out of a pasture-hill and hanged a saint?
The same that, giving birds a tale of heaven,
Could fill the space behind the lids with lies,
And throng with devils hour's careless word?
If it is so, the friend who keeps my side
Is he not apt to cause a wound of words,
Much more of iron, where I am most weak?
The sea that tells an endless tale of peace,
On whose broad breast the peaceful packet walks,
Might it not suddenly become a fiend,
Crush sleeping centuries, rock with joy at wreck?

XXII

How shall we man this mountain when it rocks,
Only by lying wait and trapping clouds?
If, as the tucket sounds, the winking winds
Would join us, we might be safe: but, no.
Young men, with terror from the lap of love,
Leap! Know in that minute the vice-locked bone,
The twining veins that stammer out their tale
Before the fleeing blood cuts off their dole.
Know that the word, the southern sound, is false,
That truth's in tendons and the sobbing heart.
For me, there'll wailing be among the elms,
And there will dirges sing about the barns.
Pie-fingering thumb pulled out my waited prize,
Gave me a grave to tend, an empty home.

XXIII

Though cities fall we cannot hold the hour
When dream-built phoenix sheltered in the leaves,
And the proud pilgrim with his marble thighs
Strode through the forest years before our birth.
It is another tale, made before sound
Prompted the patriarch behind the eyes,
While the weak globe, uncertain of his goal
Still swung in space, in matter without mould.
Yet song was there, growing through the lids,
Gradual, child-footed, wanting but the grave
To snap the leash and cast it into light.
Now cries the blood and the plucked bone cries,
And only the heart lies still as nerveless hands
Scatter the perfect years, the perfect years.

XXIV

Not drum, nor trembling tucket-sound shall stay
The falling hammer, the forgotten word;
The halting foot be fast upon the shift
And lock of laughing sand as on this rock,
Racked with the Age's weevils, pulled in parts
By a straw-haired Nemesis whose babbling blood
Scoffs in man's head and turns his heart to flint.
This is no moment for the lover's word,
When cracked-bone terror and the lurking barb
Lie in the flower's bell nor show their eyes:
O hands, O heart, how many centuries
Must we be stifled in this stony grave?
How many bloody minutes roll across
The land, before the love we bear is born?

XXV

Which is the final shape, then, which the sharp
Edge to cut from history its coat of brass
And bear unto the forty winds a sign?
Which of these voices leans on silver tongue,
Learning a weapon that will dull the sword,
And blazing stalactite reduce to dust?
Which fling my devil down and let me sleep?
Patience, my masters, while the children weep
Their unborn bodies' blood for my poor beast,
Whose shackles falter in his wordy ruin,
Whose worlds are nothing more than angels sing
From coloured pages, unbelieved, unheard
Of men. Patience again, I ask you, lest
In carving we may cut the throat of hope.

THE BOAT RETURNS

The boat had drifted, battered, to the beach
That rings my heart's deep sea, crusted with grief,
Decked as for festival with tropic flower,
A slim green lizard grinning at the prow.

What pain has spoken prophecy aboard
You, gushing from the hatch? Oh, what black sun
Has blistered your gold sides to make gold mouths?
To cry, 'O whither now, wild waves, O where?'

I saw this boat against the summer moon:
I caught her music in my summer ear:
I felt her tackle pulling in my breast:
Her prow against my heart-bone making way.

Then blood spun skywards like the frantic lark,
Speaking a language tongue had never known;
Singing an ancient song, forgotten when
Twelve sturdy Greeks pulled out to sea from Tyre.

Oh, Mistress Mine, oh, Traveller! What land
Is poorer for your leaving? What the tale
Your lips, if lips they are that crack your sides,
Could tell, in sighs between the shiftings of the tides?

And while heart spoke a circling gull called, 'Speak!'
'Speak!' croaked the raven from the ruined wharf.
'Oh, tell your tale!' the grim crab cackled. And
A thousand creatures from the sea sighed, 'Tell!'

.   .   .   .   .   .

'Long time ago, a time too proud for years,
Too great with grief to bear a century's name,
I trod, a virgin, on the sea's soft breast,
Full in my pride and stepping like a queen.

'Born in the misty heaven between the sun
And the far poles of suffering and delight,

53

Fashioned by tearful hands whose eyes sang praise,
I walked the earth's small floor on holiday. . . .

'With deck awash, and foundering under fruits,
I heard the hammer fall and saw men fall
Beneath the lash, agape with leather throats,
So that Rome's tables be complete with lime!

'I carried a pale prophet, safe in chains,
Whose crime was that inside his wagging head
A story would not cry itself to sleep —
A yarn about a madman and two thieves.

'And after time unmeasured I beheld
Tall cliffs, a hoped-for haven, white with chalk;
But rest was only iron in the heart,
And conqueror burning blue-limbed men in woods.

'From my tall tree, the pale-eyed wanderers saw
Dark men in feathers, happy under heaven,
And left them when they sailed again, plucked crows,
Black stinking bundles rolling on the shores.

'It was all waste, or woe, or blood upon my decks;
Young lovers parted by a salty dream;
Husband from wife and warm fire dragged away,
To cough inside my hold among the ice:

'Man torn from mother, father from his son,
To watch with blackening eyes the Southern Cross;
Or wait with thickening tongue while wars were won,
And dripping life, to singe King Philip's beard.

'So many years! Oh, how the time has dragged!
And not an inch of ocean not my own;
No sight unknown, from Dutchman at the Cape
To green Sargasso's serpents and their stench!

54

THE BOAT RETURNS

'So many years! So many brave bones bleached!
So many tears to swell the salt sea's dower!
And so much blood; ah, so much useless blood,
That might have relearned love, discovered God!'

.   .   .   .

But was there not a time, I whispered, when
With proud, knife-fingered boy upon your prow,
You won again your maidenhead and stepped,
Lissom as linnet through a poet's dream?

When winds brought not the message of decay,
And desks were dressed with diamond-flashing song?
When the great snowy albatross beat time,
Close in your wake, to poet's golden rhyme?

Have I not heard that as the moon sank low
Beneath the tides, strange creatures from below
Crept up your sides, and panted on your boards
To hear the magic leave the dark boy's lips?

.   .   .   .

'We danced through latitudes no chart has dreamed,
In bays reported by no map we stayed;
It seemed we sailed another globe, as though
Like thieves we crept away while men still slept.

'With this young god as steersman, many sights
I saw. I watched bergs born, heard mother's scream
As silver-blue babe toppled from the womb,
Moving the waters even to the Poles.

'I heard the many-coloured birds that speak
The language that created men from slime;
And watched the torpid serpents dreaming worlds
No eyes would see, among the rotting trees.

'Had we been mates, he boat or I a bride,
Time would have stayed for us, our legend kind.
But sap had dried within me, blood in him.
And so the morning broke when, in my sight

'The shores he had invented groaned and wept,
Heaved with a death-bed sickness, slowly shrank,
A damp, amorphous, sickening heap of filth,
Stinking to heaven, washed by a putrid sea.

'And from that minute, he whose hand had led
Leaned on my mast and let the tiller swing;
His peace polluted and his gods unmanned,
He watched the obscene seas with eyeless holes.

'Speaking no word, his tongue cracked like dry straw;
Thinking no thought, his brain like dew dissolved;
Dreaming no dream, his heart became a stone. . . .
And so my captain leaned against my mast.

'Then one night while I slept beneath the lee
Of a shadow that had come before the moon,
A tempest rose from all the dead men's throats,
Who pined for home, chill on the ocean's floor.

'I woke in anguish from my desert-dream
And heard the thunder crackling in my hold;
All emptiness I felt, no one to love.
And by the dawn I found my love had gone.

'And in his place an ancient thing I found,
Gaunt as the love that madness bears for peace,
Deaf, blind and helpless, lying on my decks,
Waiting for death since this red world began.

'And as the years wore thin, I learned to hear
The reed-weak whimperings that seemed to crawl,

56

Faint as a pauper's joy, from this sad ape,
Words that no ear might trap but nearing death:

'*I see him trading metal rods for pearls;*
Spitting on verses in some sunny town:
I see him trading pearls for women's limbs;
And burning sonnets as the sun goes down.

'*I see him, wild with wine, in narrow streets,*
Creating ways of passion for a friend:
I see him, sad and sleepless in a cell,
Weeping that justice cannot slay with fire.

'*But, last of all, upon a rusty bed,*
Troubled with flies and noises from the docks,
I hear him shrieking as his thick blood turns,
"Where lies she now! Oh, where my lovely bark?" '

'I listened softly, stilled the rocking waves
With my broad bosom and my oaken strength;
I waited breathless, like a heated maid
For raping whisper, but no whisper came.

'And then, in anger with this weary thing,
Impatiently I swung my shoulders, flapped
The tatters of my mast-head, asked again.
But all I heard was shark's disgusted scream. . . .

'So now you find me, sheltering in this shore,
Away from tempest and the sad-eyed boy
Whose fingers still reach out across the seas,
Across the blood that's washed my creaking boards.'

.   .   .   .   .   .

And will you stay? I asked the tired boat,
And bear the sea's sweet harvest to the world?
And will you stay, I asked, that poets may
Find rest for once upon your hallowed breast?

'That may not be,' I thought the words came back,
'For I am weary and my heart is old. . . .'
The tower-clock spoke night, and as I watched,
The wailing bark sank silently from sight.

POEMS FROM A WORK IN PROGRESS

I

In the spinster room where came no birth or death,
Above the strife, my linnet-hours I spent.
For many days my dancing eyes had sucked
A message from the death mask on the wall:
The craggy features, chin like cloven oak,
The bolted prison mouth and shuttered eyes
Forced words, but offered none: the brow beat
Back my fingers' kisses, stopped my mouth.

Today I cracked these shackles; with my lath
Lashed into frenzy, broke the brazen arm
That tricked my tickle-brain under a cloak,
Sped like a winter-pleasure to the room
Where Nemesis upon his niche held fast:
Smashed back the blind cast, and choked with dust.

II

I snatched the shape of visions in a dream
Dreaming a land of visions as I walked:
And by my hip love's angel paced in black,
And through my head a devil pranked in white
Trod in a trance, forgot to bare his blade
And crop the dangling fruit his boy's eyes loved.
My feet were doves, all silvered in my tears,
My swift hands fishes, salmon of the moon,
And from my globe of words a scarlet rose
Measured me problem's patterns like an eye.
My sable sideman smiled, bidding me stay
With known, and let the unsought cipher rot:
Yet, waking from his circled·heaven, my ape
With scorching diamonds beguiled my doves.

59

III

So it was fated: set upon a hill
Lay palm-high wizards buried in a stone,
Nourished by raven's descant, by the trees'
Gaunt question of the winter moon. At dawn
An ice-age slumber clove their thorny tongues
And silence, stiff as candles round a corpse,
Armoured their feeble flame. This hill I clomb
Ere cock-crow scratched his wiry niche in clouds:
Alms-can, my saviour, mumbled in my clutch
A song of sorrow. Like a wraith I stepped.
Knock. 'No word will come,' the black word came.
Knock, knock. 'Ask the raven as he drinks
Your vine-drops.' 'Ask the echo, ask the trees,
We are dying, dead.' Knock . . . knock.

IV

There is a tree within a spinning seed
Inside a stiff mole's head. Sir Craven Hawk,
He of the five-knifed hand, from out his tower,
Comes me a-coursing on a summer morn.
Boltwise he droppeth down upon the green
Blood of earth, snuffing the sexton's friend.
Now, with a sigh, as who should say what flesh!
Pinion unfolds and brothers turret wisps,
Until my ape, envy of kite as kith,
Kins me with gesture, shouts into my mouth,
'Look up! He's out of sight!' My ticking dial
Now mocks me with a song whose chorus cries:
'Within the mole, the seed, and on the tree
Burgeoned the blossom that you dreamt to drag!'

V

Then voice came to me from the land of bones:
'As water unstable nor shalt thou excel,
Though thou hast raiment plucked from empire's ruin,
Lashed into stony places, to the leopard's lair,
The morning's minions, children of the sky;
And country-colours, safe as old crone's hand,
Witched into winter-grey and left boughs bones.'
So my dream ended, I from the visions fled
Into the fields alone, nor did my box
Mansion a mammon, nor stepped my side-man light
Into the light of mourning. I was alone!
And as I raised my eyes the roses shrank,
Covering with petal's mist my moving feet.
Upon the glistening grass lay two dead doves.

VI

Above the clotted clouds a riding bird
Mounts over man: shuddering, his shade
Clouds like forgotten dreams the mind of mole
Safe under sod: the wiry hand makes sign
Of recognition through the soil. So man,
Feeling the future's shade across the plain,
Huddles in darkness, listens to the lap
Of purple channel in the brother's vein,
Hating his fear, sharing his unthought dread,
Afraid to move or look, fearing the word.
After the storm the scavenger flies home
To rocky ruin in among the crags:
The mole awakes and mumbles over graves:
And man takes up the sword, forgets to love.

VII

Taking my tired heart in wizened hands
I wept: wept to the nodding banners left
Where the cold knife broke the dusky gold
For bread; wept to the patient brother mole,
Making his bed a thousand worlds away
From needle eyes that kill the flower they kiss.
Only the flint swung in my echoing cave
Could keep me manwise, head against the stars:
Only the magic of a pear-tree dream,
Before lust's eagle urged my hankering limb,
The small voice whispering dusty rooms, years
Before sunlight picked the lock that baffled sight,
Only that music tautened strings and stays
And kept me rigid while my ruin prowled.

VIII

In my starlit history bright moths
Like lace-frail hands beside a shadowed grave
Grew from my dreams. Hear by the word their wings
Hatch in the quiet violet's veils of fantasy
My trembling hand halt edge and fluttering up
Share brotherhood with branch. The dying year
Bequeathed me bones in iron scroll, left home
A heap of ashes where the adder's brood
No native brook, mandrake where roses lay,
Only a nettle-welcome to a corpse's prayer.
But these last nights, lean as a pauper's cur,
Meagre, are meat enough to clothe the sticks
I cherish. Out from the star-decked branches, moths
Wander their way like music through a mist.

IX

The trinket hour set in a century's foil
Etched love and laughter in my itching bone,
And spun a warp that wound my phoenix round.
The day of sunlight grew a beard of musk
And centaury, incenséd in pavilion
Shot its bright bolts inside my portalled dream.
Deep in a forest like a giant's hair
The twilit trolls danced madness into peace
And plucked the godhead's golden minutes like
Bright plums. There dwelt a maiden, fair
In the flesh, but rotten in the womb. Her hand
Shed daggers as a death drops tears.
Wreathing a flowered pattern through my sleep,
Feet wrought a pathway to her golden doom.

X

Sir Lancelot, between the thighs I smirked.
(Sticks in the golden rushes O). My lance
Showed me the pathway, loud wound my horn my words
Into the shell. (Ask of the frozen stone!)
Sir Fatherfast, under the silken sheet
My trade I plied nor prayed to plight a troth,
Only that she into the black night's sleeve
Should rede me riddles, unlock the dumb bell's tongue.
(Ask of the stone, I say.) The morrow's morn,
Minstrel I moneyed, knowing his string-delight,
Knowing the gilded finger point a way
Up hill or down. (Ask till the stone falls blind!)
Lanceless I left, leaving my wounded horn
Behind in bower, seeking the mouths of stone.

XI

Rushing like Eloi over broken homes
With tongue of bones, the streaming hair
Of truth lashes my eyes to iron, and sinks
Under the giant-mould my gasping globe.
Hung on a hill for birds, my naked head
Whistles the word the truant wind holds best,
While strands that swung a blade, gaunt as tree,
Bride to the Northern Lights, the sacred bread
Spat by a pilgrim in his forest way,
Falls in the feathered palace like a shell,
Blows the grim yarning grandam from the door
Of hope. Beneath the warping board, a root
Thrusts a frail finger into worlds we loved,
Shows how tomorrow tires of our dreams.

XII

A vixen's lair, laid in the tomb of a prince
Lures my mind's madness sweetly. In its ruin
Love flaunts his singing tatters as a robe
And robs the public rose to prank his hair;
Even the lamb of God in truth can see
How paupers strut to glory over dung.
Across the mourning hills the swallow's scream
Brays brazen, like hell's trumpet. In my ears
The red blood roars, sour as a childhood dream,
While never more near than hope, my fingers' silk
Paints Christ across my angel chrysalis.
But, with a virgin's wink, the rusting string
Snaps in a hand, frail as a broken bird . . .
Leaves empty years to tempt an iron tongue.

XIII

I have shrunk startled at the scream of moths
In autumn ivy, have tottered as with stealth
The pauper wren, wrapped in my woolly blood,
Knocked on my heart for comfort in the cold.
Was there a man whose hands like silver knives
Cropped mercy from an apple-tree in spring,
Cut to the frozen bone the fruits of peace
And shot with words love's linnets as they flew?
Perhaps in my breast the vinegar still creeps
That nourished such a man, from whose eyes
The selfsame bitter message moves. Horror
Should with crimson mouth make woe if such
Is truth. But stay, my hand before my face
Holds not the gathered flowers, but five bright swords!

XIV

When gods doubt days and out of red see ruin,
Who stands amongst us, ready for his end?
When dog bites dog, and devil with his nail
Undoes the hopes of sexton, flouts the wren
And scatters dust upon the hallowed sticks,
Who shall give answer, who with rotting tongue
Broider sweet systems, cites juvenate?
Under the whoring eyes of stars, winking
I waited Death's knock in my heart of ice,
Hindered the patient worm upon his quest,
Found only this beneath the lichened stone;
'The toad's skull split, no amethyst is found,
(What ducat can man coin from haloed head?)
Nor are there pockets in a pauper's shroud.'

XV

The toppled town forgets the kiss of musk
At moth-time, skull demands the simpler scent
Of earth, and in the purple heaven of princes
Only a shade shoves lepers from the board.
Drunk with the ichor wrung from aching eyes,
The spirit totters, tattered, sport of winds
Blowing where they list through the dark mind.
Rusting in dew, the fleshless sword, ghost
In a corner, watches the falcon's midnight glee.
This is a tale of ruin, writ in a wasted
Year. The haggard children creeping from
My hand's despair, turn eyes like dying flowers
To bid good-day: their wizened leaves of hands
Flutter like wings, and groan, and then lie still.

XVI

'The alabaster name in numbered word
Shall, in a dungeon-darknes, drain to death;
Love's diamond in a red alembic mock
Mouther, the moon, and tawny wind force cloud
And leaf, the summer's brother, out of breath.
Mountain unto mountain, each to each,
Move manwards through the world nor take no heed
Of Nemesis with thunder in his cap,
Whose finger, foul as hawk, despises love,
But picks the flowered blood unto the bone
And in the stony socket bawds his tongue.
Heed have ye! In the silken tent let sword
Before portal stretch his wary limb. Care
Shall with sharper nail kill larger fowl!'

XVII

Bell-mouth! if madman words were rope I'd swing,
And few the silver tears get from you!
I taste the track your double wind blows now,
I've tumbled to your crows decked out as doves:
And I can tell you, hell across my heart,
That first time out along the razor-crag
I see your shape, fall to your knees and beg
The snake to snick with quicker knife than mine!
But there I go, flailing the velvet world
With brittle sticks, and none to hear my word.
Out in the street I feel the voice of man
Pluck coldness from a stone unto his heart,
While in my reeling room the flowers' eyes
Follow my every move, my every sigh.

XVIII

Doom in the bell, and blood upon the flower
Twitches my feeble sticks: inside my ear
A devil crouches, muttering of the night.
His viper-words like velvet stroke my brain
To frenzy, words that are swords and worse than steel:
'Out of a land of eyes came first a priest
Sweet with a snake's desire, upon whose head
The future's thunder thatched a flaming mane
Of godshaped falsehood from a flower's bell,
Which minion, muffled by his swinging lute,
Laid bare the villages with silken saws
And left upon the boughs in place of fruit
His son, untimely ripped from future's tomb:
Go ye! Do likewise, ere the glass shall run!'

XIX

Now Time has painted dearth across my heart,
And those are coral that were once my eyes,
I sit, watching the winter's breath upon
The pane. Under a cloven cloak, a man
Offers his twitching twigs for my poor crumbs.
Is it my father? Beneath his rags a bone
Box grins riddles from its wormy holes.
I see a stone swinging on hempen cords
Between his cage's bars, where no bird sings.
My loaf he takes, he takes my love of life
Under his creeping tatters, forked to his side.
I shudder as I watch my father's hairs
Drop ants and scorpions; shudder as I find
My fleshbare fingers folding over ants.

XX

White-eyed, the questing tiger slides his length
Beneath my graveyard sheet, and as I smile
My ears grow friendly to the scream of moles.
Love and let thrive, I tell my brother box,
Is lightning mine that lusting lads should crave
And drag their desert-longing four winds' ways,
While I, stroking a penance out of prickly stars,
Have power to give, have will to shed my gold?
The moon with inmate grimace moves her lips
And shows my words are winged. A tree nods,
Nudges his cousin owl and sings a storm:
Out on the plain I hear a bird's applause.
Soil falls, wood warps, a pauper muscle moves:
I smell a voice: 'The spade!' it shrieks, 'The spade!'

XXI

That is the answer, that the last shape of truth:
The final minute no man's history is
But his, and from his box no word may wind
Its seagreen treachery about the ears
Of shapes, mourning the passing of a shape.
From the dry sticks no gushing oil can leap
Into their frozen hearts and coin them gold.
They are alone, knowing not who they are,
Or whom the misty stranger in their midst:
They are alone, feeling no pain but theirs,
Knowing not whose is lot to brother next
The six-foot cedar swinging through the ground.
All they can hear are echoes from the roots,
A voice that screams of spades, and then is still.

DEATH MASK

Hid by the stone stare, I dreamt a fox
With bloody beard: the sneering lip
Spring-hung, to kiss my hand with fang
Before the clicking second's foot could flee:
Back from the nostril's grin I watched a flower
Wither and groan, fall black upon the patient floor.

Through many dreams this hanging drum of wax
Followed my motion, waiting a slip
It seemed; and days, however long,
Led always to the dusty room, where he
Watched. By day and on the hills the power
Slept; but moon would always find him at the door.

So the thread wound: joy snapped like elder sticks,
Brittle in winter. The thunder's clap
In silence plagued my mind; song
Shrank in the caverns of my heart. He
Tempted, till my hands snatched in their fear,
Only a spider's web, brain to the mocking leer.

SEE-SAW ON DYING

The bent-bone muscle spent the sacked heart
Nightly neigh their pain as my mind's rats gnaw
Down to the swinging stone my soul my flower
Clutched in the claw, ground in the jaw of living:
My pain, the noise that midnight nothing makes,
    Stiff silence shrieking from a polar hell:
(Alas! bent bone and muscle spent are dumb.)

The watered blood swings slowly in the heat
My sacked heart cracked heart drives upon a spur
Of hope of love of living from the fear
Of death of coffin-scratch of black mole-wooing.
Come, break the bones death, crunch them till the shrieks
They sculpt in hell's air (all hope's lull)
Dwindle in the ice-black tomb.

THE SEASONS

The sound of summer is the sound of sorrow,
When heaven's outcast falls before the door.
The sound of summer is the sigh of horror,
When the thin scarecrow knows his heart of straw

Shall never flicker to the starling's chatter:
His dry arms droop as dropping sparrows hover.
When brothel-brawling Spring displays his fangs
(Yesman to summer and sin's yoke-fellow)
The raven shrieks with anger. His red wings
Wrinkle the lake he crosses, shake the willow-
Herb fan-dance among the river-sallows,
Drive him at once to strike and mate with swallows.

Twelve months of ice and stone is winter's stature,
Fugue-built, we know him, of twisted bone and vein,
Kingly and kindly, yet not without misfeature.
But should this emblem randy in his ruin,
Delve for the ducat in my skull, nature
Should cry 'usury' on the sorry creature.
Yes, worse than Winter, with his sable armour,
Is the rain-failer, gobbet-grasping season,
The smiling hatchet-man, second-season mummer,
Whose harvests burn, whose bee-bag's load is poison.
O, heart's bells roar around the bloody haven,
'Where lies my peace, when thus my year lies cloven?'

EMPEROR ZERO ON DEATH

Where lies the truth I touted years for, I,
Emperor Zero, slain between altar and sanctuary?
My golden blood, lacing the marble steps,
Blinks in the sun, creeps between crevices
To find in rats' remains a lovelier lie
Than that it flowed for first. Sweet 'pothecary
Civet and centaury held in full-thighed laps,
The paps, the lips and all the queenly faces

71

Bred in our own or other's time are naught,
Truth's sweetness, so-called, naught beside this peace.
Yet I have hated death and feared him too,
Figured him out to be the mean old man
Whose bomb caught ladies taking off their skirt,
Shore between lovers locked beneath the sheets;
Who left men speechless; like the mindless snow,
Built barricades between your home and mine.

But now I know him, know that his pictured pain
Is only paper-talk; the left he swings is fake;
Being forgotten's just the only hell.
Death, when you've once smacked off his witless face,
Is no more than a wet page in the rain,
The midnight noise that empty rooms may make,
Or silence screaming from a horned sea-shell.
So, leave this truth stuff, boys, and walk right in!

THE HOMELESS

There is no home: only the rotten stick,
The sodden thatch, are there.
As wind winks the rusty latch
Clanks, and silence groans
Above the stairs. Listen,
It is a footstep, come to tell
The listeners there is no home.

As I made my way through the world
I heard as from a million-fathom bed
The voice of history, all men's story:
Saw the cloaked sword and heard it speak
A tongue of passion and of pain:
Heard age in armour hurrying to war,

Voiceless, its wrinkled claw unsheathed
But strengthless; its white hair bare
But cold. There were words and words
But none told truth. Walking alone
I heard these things and saw these things,
Yet nothing knew, nor knew a word.

There is no home: only a weed-grown track
Leads past the adder's lair.
Wreathe me, with scabia and with vetch,
A crown, and with these stones
Build hope a cairn.
Old shapes have fled, the house is still.
My heart sobs, 'There is no home.'

POEM FOR EASTER

Twelve-tongued, the bell Hosannah paints a grave,
Swung in the claws of vultures. Over dead seas
The message slides, rams its unwavering word
Through worm-clogged sockets; cleaving the womb of woe,
Shows, like a child untimely ripped, the blood
That masks the glory of a birth: but eyes,
Tasting the future's shape feel on the reed
Not vinegar, but swelling grape. The nail
Flames through the world of darkness like a sword.

It was a black beginning when the dove,
Spiked in the breast, fell frozen through the boughs
Into the poacher-pocket. The stiff lord
Dangled from a fence, his thorny eye
Shed peace, they say. The blustering tribal god

73

Had other business on that day, alas!
That was a pox of pages in the dead
Past. But watch the fled fears on next week's reel;
See how the promise blossoms. Lo, a bird!

PSALM CARVED FROM SORROW

An ocean wags my tomb-tied tongue,
From caverned depths dead eyes in coils stare out:
'Look, angel, how the column sways,
Rocks in the raven's passing wing.
Under the mother-hill a Christmas town
Shudders in starlight. This shall be night
When shambling god, whose flowered fang
Taps weasel's eggs and coffined pride, bought
In a kingdom's labour, yearly dies.
Unlace your helmet, then, and sing
Psalms carved from sorrow, heaven's mountains lurch,
Fling Satan from his summit into light.'

But wordless dreams cast down to wail
Like little Hugh of Lincoln in the night,
Starve on my doorstep. In my praise
The purple psalm of hell they sing
And none to stop their bloody mouths till dawn:
'The King of Spain his daughter, dight
With maid's desire for gold, long
Lusted after more than nutmeg brought,
A mere pear! Come, dry those eyes:
Look past the turret where they wing,
The screaming spearhead making for the marsh.
Cloud's hounds all-hail you in their flight!'

THE POET

In my hand's seven scrivening bones
A message strides in wordy greaves;
In my priest-hole heart a knife
Cuts the pages of love's griefs.
Sea-wind and mountain-wind in my elms
Nail to my house-wall unfilled graves,
And choral clock beats time to moles
Processing darkly through sleep's groves.

The wilderness that hides my head
Hides eagle's heart in sparrow's coat;
The coffin swinging in my ribs
Was carved from oak that bore a boat;
The monkish pages of my blood
In werewolf moonlight mock the sweet
Movement of my willow-hands,
As God walks with me in the street.

'I LOCKED LOVE'S DOOR'

I locked love's door, and bade my brother seek
Bread in the byre and song among the kine.
I closed his eyes, stone-pillared in their Winter
And doled with last year's hopes a threadbare crow
To troll him dirge; meet requiem, a merry mode
I ordered, for the laughing lad whose gods
Coined the red leaves and sat in Satan's chair,
Or with a whisper filched a city's heart,
But never budged a bone when famine prowled.

What wrong was it I wrought? As I returned
Strewing the churchyard ashes in my way
For fancy's sake, I saw a wrinkled child,
Who watched with orphan-eye my path to peace,
Who screamed and vanished from my father-hand.

IN SUCH A WILDERNESS AS THIS

(For Nicholas Moore)

In such a wilderness as this
Judas, my Judas, what birds?
The thin wren, whose jewelled eye
Slips like a pick-purse hand between
The vulture and his fancy, finds
Only a workhouse stone. Swallow,
Sweet sister, choreography neglects
To stoop above the sparrow's ort,
To glide about the smoky heap
For dung-straw left by hands
Wizened before the year had clutched his heart.
(It is all old and dry and better left unsaid.)

But Judas, speak before the wish
Wrinkles, before the cloud's
Cankered teeth toss lightnings through
My rags, burnish the creaking bone.
This, in a graveyard hour, sends
Passion packing: 'Blood will follow
Blood. One sword in no wise acts
A flower-token in the heart
Of dreamer.' Is it the part of hope
To challenge with painted wands
The mountain-gesture, spit the rebel earth
At sunset while it dozes, Judas, strike it dead?

REMEMBERING LAST YEAR

The worn hand of the year with rusty key,
With mother-gesture in her fading eye,
This night has opened up a box of tears:
My urchin eyes have goggled as they dropped,
Small empty battles, tragedies of sticks;
My emperor hands, too stern to play the maid
And pander to the suckling in my blood,
Too soft to shut out memory from the eyes,
Pluck penance out of roses to their ruin,
Hang by my sword, afraid to stark her blade.
Urchin and ancient, stand I in my grief
Watching a younger season's frolics, fears,
Feeling again the fresh wind from the hills,
And the small thorn like spearhead in my breast.

POEM FOR CHRISTMAS

Ned Time, the dragon-toothed, he, shadow on the wall,
No babe might brave. Shunned is he through the length of land,
As scriptural fury leaping in a five-knifed hand,
Woe-worker, Herod's-henchman. The Christ's thin wail
His bloodhound-homage fetches free, and with the oath
He cozened at the cards from Death, both worlds he leaves,
Pot-luck to practise, steps stablewards and vanquished moves
As still as frosty-morning's shivering grasses' breath.

Bright vespers in the fire flare, whispers in the byre:
'Is this the promised poppet or a barnyard brat?
Knowledge is owed us now whose heels have crossed the hills.
'Say on, for we must know: shall this bright baby here
From dark tree dangle bleeding, earth-scorned heaven-fruit;
This lamb, lap's minion, swing, shriven with three nails?'

THE THREE SELVES

(*For Donald Foster*)

The beast whose heartbeats echo in my own
Is no man's enemy but mine;
Whose murderous words and worthless tears
Pluck from my strings alone their traitor tune,
Tear from my angel lips alone a midnight groan.

Yet we are fellows: born of one rutting rib,
We know one darkness, follow one star;
And should Death wake us, the same curt word
Would shake Time's corridors with shrieks of fear,
Topple both vein-strung scaffolds, in the red moment rob.

Then who should save us? Not the gutter god
We sneered at, nor the laws we fought,
Nor my fiend's fangs, nor my right arm.
(My Caesar died, alas, before the night
Had whispered saving secrets to my wide-eyed lad.)

Which rising man, who holds my cup of tears
Waiting to drink, is puppy-blind;
Urchin to friend and foe he stands
Cozening history. What difference shall he find
Between the end he loves, the backstairs fate he fears?

WINTER 1939

In this frost-time pilfering plover
Finds none for brother. Fieldweed sprouts
Like stubble on a corpse, and jawshut door
That through the love-years leaned on latch,
Now grips his greeting in the lock.
Fly high, delve deep heart, you'll not find

The freeword rafternested that you knew:
Even pert saucerclack upon the cup is heard
By muffled agent in the byre,
And oakgrained leatherleg, along the lanes,
Starts over shoulder, shocked, at falling leaf.

What then your secret, lackland lover?
Fly there in fallen-feather notes
No ear but countryear has heard before,
Wings time that none before could watch?
Where do you travel, foam-and-black;
Leads weedlocked tunnel where; what end
The worldwar find you, stream? I grew
In halls a daggerdream no eye nor heart had feared,
Where loglove forced the kiss of fire
Even; trojan-travail prospered; bairns
Before door sprawled, love in the heart of life.

The book closes; nor can joy ever
Tap, tendril-tender, to the beats
Of waiting lover heart, upon his door.
Outside, wrapping the sorrowing wretch,
Devil-faced mists mumble, flock
Terror-screaming martlets, wind
Wakes childbed horrors, teeth gnaw
A way for nightmare through the creaking board.
Tongue stumbles; in their fear
The feeble winghands flutter on the horns
Of madness, kissing the flower-fashioned knife.

THE OLD ONES

The old ones knew that black was hate,
White garment purity and red one sin;
They spoke the language of the trees
And opened veins to let love in.

These old ones, feeling life was brief
And brittle as the fire-baked shard,
Could find no seat for sentiment,
So mended weakness with a sword.

In them the heart was made of gold,
But mind was forged of steel so sharp
That hand which plucked the harp could shape
From father's skull a drinking cup.

The old ones' fashion we have lost,
Whose red is passion, white deceit;
In casting devil from the flesh,
Who perish with the bread we eat.

AGE

Age is the act of being held by life
A minute after Death has passed the door
To walk a neighbouring street and thrust his love,
Bitter as burning leaves, upon another.

It is the state of seeing in a fire
Not passion but a shield against the cold;
Not scent or colour in a garden flower,
But sign that soil still has the will to yield.

The threat of age lies in an oaken box
Carried at moonlight by black-coated men;
Even the harmless knock of roadman's pick
Plucks at the fear that day comes not again.

Oh, pity, that this melancholy song
Should echo down the seasons into Spring!

THE BLACK BOOK

(*For Conroy Maddox*)

Pacing the pages of the midnight book
I see the pale man fingering a skull,
And the old dog snuffing at his heels,

A bleeding hand probes underneath the vetch,
Violates the garb of gothic for a prize,
And comes to light clutching five black eggs.

A sneering eye is staring through the pane:
It is a future come to mock a past;
The Landseer turns towards the wall for shame.

Under the roof a cripple carves a bowl;
No cough can keep him from the swarming roads,
Touching his cap for alms from riding lords.

Beneath the floor a lime-dried corpse sits up
And, listening to the after-dinner talk,
Fumbles the dagger in his linen cloak.

Hidden by trees, the boy engraves a stone
With threats as old as mountains in the West.
He sees the white head crumble from his wrath.

Where the grey monuments are set in rows
A faceless figure chuckles in no hand.
No cock shall crow before this deed is done!

Orgiastic emblems flute across the winds,
Seven seasons wind the tired globe along;
The page blows over — and the poem ends.

SONNET

Black the wind wailing in the future's voice
And the broken years falling piece by piece;
The only music, hope in empty skull
And the old ones crying, crying under the hill.

Come morn or evening, it shall be the same,
The same feet moving in their wounded rhyme;
Nor may it change till men do, never while
The unborn listen to the dead tongue's tale.

The young boy took a knife and cut the tree,
Then carved his weapon from the springing bough;
But winter and the father sacked the sap
And struck the salmon as he made his leap.

So, deep in caverns you can hear them sing,
These eyeless who cannot remember Spring.

RELICS

In that stone head, obscenity
Has been preserved a thousand years;
A bible-leaf of families
Have shuddered at the pointed ears.

The sword that hangs upon the wall
Is notched the length of its long blade,
And children at the village school
Dream of the trusses it has mowed.

Close against the lichened tower
Still lives a witch. Around her head
She wears a shawl, and white as flour
Her lips count every step she treads.

But when the dusk-born lovers stand
The figure sobs, 'Oh where's my soul?'
The sword sighs for the long-dead hand,
The old hag huddles from the owl.

BIRDWATCHER

Between decision and ensuing act
Tosses a world of pain. Hope's brittle twig
Swings in the muscles' bitter wind, and soul,
Like frightened bird, clamps down his claw
And, wings shut fast about him, waits the fall.
Below, there sits the fox, whose name is death;
Above, a plum hangs loose, which is delight.
And in the meantime the intolerable wind
Blows faith and fear in alternating bursts.

The lonely watcher sheltered under rock
Smiles at the obvious end. The bird is blind.
Tomorrow crows will pick his rattling wings;
And higher up the hill a man in red
Will blood his boy and carry home the brush.

THE MAGIC WOOD

The wood is full of shining eyes,
The wood is full of creeping feet,
The wood is full of tiny cries:
You must not go to the wood at night!

I met a man with eyes of glass
And a finger as curled as the wriggling worm,
And hair all red with rotting leaves,
And a stick that hissed like a summer snake.

The wood is full of shining eyes,
The wood is full of creeping feet,
The wood is full of tiny cries:
You must not go to the wood at night!

He sang me a song in backwards words,
And drew me a dragon in the air.
I saw his teeth through the back of his head,
And a rat's eyes winking from his hair.

The wood is full of shining eyes,
The wood is full of creeping feet,
The wood is full of tiny cries:
You must not go to the wood at night!

He made me a penny out of a stone,
And showed me the way to catch a lark
With a straw and a nut and a whispered word
And a pennorth of ginger wrapped up in a leaf.

The wood is full of shining eyes,
The wood is full of creeping feet,
The wood is full of tiny cries:
You must not go to the wood at night!

He asked me my name, and where I lived;
I told him a name from my Book of Tales;
He asked me to come with him into the wood
And dance with the Kings from under the hills.

The wood is full of shining eyes,
The wood is full of creeping feet,
The wood is full of tiny cries:
You must not go to the wood at night!

But I saw that his eyes were turning to fire;
I watched the nails grow on his wriggling hand;
And I said my prayers, all out in a rush,
And found myself safe on my father's land.

Oh, the wood is full of shining eyes,
The wood is full of creeping feet,
The wood is full of tiny cries:
You must not go to the wood at night!

THE CRIMSON CHERRY-TREE

There is no sweeter sight, I swear, in Heaven
Than blossom on the cherry-trees by Clee.
Ah dainty brides, you dance on through my dreams
And in the town bring memory of a breeze
That blew from Corvedale, down the valley that
Must have run red with agony when Owen spoke,
Torturing the air about his council-chair
With shapes of fiery dragons, flaming wolves
That ran through city gates to bring despair
Upon the tow-haired marchers, tearing sheep
And leaving foul the water-holes. I feel
The failure of a people when that wind
Howls through my heart and shows me Caradoc
Heaped high with lads who should have brought their songs
Right to the walls of Ludlow, over Severn,
Regaining the green pastures with a word.

Ah cherry-tree, so lissom in the wind,
Matter for poets and the love-sick mad,
I see your virgin blossom splashed with blood,
Bright red against the white, and at your feet
The gentle prince who walked without a sword,
Believing tales of peace among the hills,
Trusting the word, the signatory name,
Forgetting the black seasons of a race.

THE LOST ONES

(*For Robert Herring*)

I

It is evening and the wounded sun
Throws its red road across the sea;
A road of blood across a lake of glass,
Deeper than love, clearer than death,
Still as a feather upon lifeless lips;
Calm and mysterious as glass.

A red road treading to the edge of time,
To the islands that tremble on the edge
Of the dying earth. Back to the Isles
Where the red folk lived and red blades sang,
And love grew green among the rocks
Like preciously fantastic fruit.

And standing on this shore I hear
The old songs and the ancient tongues
Curling and coiling back across the years,
Along the road made by the sun,
Patiently suffering through history;
I look down deep into the lifeless glass
And catch the fleeting shadows of a sail.

II

Under the black rock as the moon comes out
Cries a seal.

The gentle eyes are lifted to my face;
The gentle voice

Flies like a deep-sea curlew through
The coral forests

Deep below the surface of the sea,
Deep, deep green.

A woman's voice wails under the black rock
And calls to me.

My eyes are blind with tears, my searching arms
Reach out in love.

But only the black rock glistens in the moon.
The green pool stirs.

III

I hear them in my bed and at my board,
The friendly folk all singing up the glen.
I hear a race's sadness in the word
That floats back to the world of weary men.

Harpers and pipers in gallant cloaks of gold,
A man and his maiden crossing the bleak moor;
And over the harsh heather the wind blows cold,
As the shock-headed peasant bolts his door.

IV

Where falcon flies above the crags
     My heart flies too;

Where fallow deer slips in the scree,
     There falls my hope;

The hand that bares the fire-lit blade,
     It is my own;

The finger that pulls tight the string
     Wears my own ring;

The tongue that sings the ancient song
Tells my own tale;

That moves a mountain in its pride,
It is my love.

V

Two lovers sat beneath the moon
All night in their cockle-boat;
They heard the lonely grey seal croon
And watched the green weed float.

Their tears streamed down as warm as blood,
Their kiss was cold as ice;
But they dreamed the dream of the broken word
And shrank from each-other's eyes.

VI

The old man pulled his tattered plaid about him and said, in the sing-song voice of the hills, 'Yes, to be sure I can tell you, for I am the only one left that can remember them. And who shall know the way their tale goes when I am gone from the hills?'

The silver shilling lay small in his brown hand, like a pool of fresh water among the tortured rocks on the shore.

'Listen, man,' he whispered. And I listened, hearing the wild, thin wind scything the purple heather, roaring like a devil across the pit between our hill and the Black Mountain; hearing the lost lamb bleating down in the valley, among the damp rocks; hearing the vixen cough and the tempestuous eagle screaming with hunger; and hearing the cold mountain-streams trickling down their gullies, over the forgotten graves of waiting warriors.

'Tell me now,' I said. 'The wind is cold and these hands are no longer my own.'

'Wait, my son,' he said, 'and let me warm you.'

Then the old man took both of my icy hands in his own and breathed upon them. A molten fire leapt through them, up along my arms to my heart, and a new gladness came over me. We crouched in the shelter of a cairn so that the wind blew over our heads, and my heart was now at peace within me.

'Listen again, man,' whispered the old man, 'And tell me what you hear.'

'I hear nothing, old man,' I said. 'The world has gone from me now. Begin, for my head is light with the silence of the hills.'

First there was nothing only emptiness, and then a voice awoke and spoke to me out of the day before any sun rose, from the shadowy land that was there when all the world was water, out of the time before history, when words were made by the birds and poems rode upon the bitter winds:

'First came the Little Folk,
Black with the plague of Desire,
Bringing their stone swords
And speaking with words of flint.

I watched them come, I saw them go!

Out to the Islands they fled,
Screaming their thorny songs,
Weaving their stony spells,
And chuckling in their hearts of flint.

I watched them go, the others come!

These were the men with the golden heads,
Brave as the eagle, fickle as the wren,
Harping and singing all the way to death.
Bright in the firelight their daughters stood,
Gold bracelets jingling on their golden arms.
Bright in the sunlight their young men stepped
To glory on the rocks, and falling lay
Bright on the sea-bed, on the clean white sand.

Swift as they came, so did they go!

90

And then the sun drew back and left the land;
The hills were empty and the caves were bare.
Only the wolves sang when the winter pinched,
And frozen seals were washed up on the shore.

But this night ended and a new day came.

Then in the summer with the sun
Came men with heads as red as fire,
And swords far keener than the Pictish flints,
But tongues as slow as dying glaciers.

And what are swords when dark men come
To build up stones and turn the red men back,
To steal the women from their beds
And lock cold iron on their hands?

What use are heads as red as flame
When golden heads could weave a spell,
And when the Small Folk from the Isles
Come back in winter with the starving wolves?

I wept to see them bleeding on the plains.'

I heard the old man sobbing at my side. My eyes were closed
as I listened to his story and to protect his pride I kept them shut.

And then his wailing stopped and back into my head rushed
all the noises of the winter hills. I heard the vixen cackling at the
kill, the lamb's brief testament, the eagle's scream as with a rush
of pinions he ascended once again into the solitude of bare-bone
winds. . . .

I looked for the old man, but he was gone. Only his frozen song
lay in my memory, the ice-cold piece of silver in my palm. . . .

VII

Through seven days and seven nights
Upon the winter sea
The white sail rode among the ice;
The boy sang merrily.

Through seven days and seven nights
The dank weed kissed the keel;
And in the white sail's whiter wake
There swam a wailing seal.

And when the nets were full with fish
The boat turned to the Isles.
The boy found weed like maiden's hair
Among the silver scales.

VIII

BOAT BLESSING

Sail whiter than the bosom of a Queen,
I cherish you;

Keel sharper than a conqueror's sword,
I love you;

Bows brighter than the hawk's bright beak,
I adore you;

Flanks frailer than a maiden's troth,
I fear you!

IX

BARD'S LAMENT

This breast which rests a harp
Should rest a sword;
These two nimble legs that leap,
Lie under sward!

I tore a music from my soul,
A shroud of sound across the hall;
I gave my heart for wheaten bread
And laughed to see the bright tears shed!

I plucked the plaint of the scarlet blade
And smiled to see the dance they made;
I stroked my strings to a song of love,
Knelt for my pence and took my leave.

But in the forest yesterday
A bird told how, when I went away,
The chief's fair daughter put on black
And died for love that turned not back.

This breast which rests a harp
Should rest a sword;
These two nimble legs that leap,
Lie under sward!

X

BLIND BARD

My heart is an acre of sandy heath
And a copse where the wild geese rest;
And a tumbling barn where kings have slept,
And a ploughshare pocked with rust.

My head is a plain as vast as the East,
Where the winds of the spirit howl,
As the prince of my dream meets his princely death
Out of the poisoned bowl.

XI

THE HEROES

(*A Winter evening; three old shepherds meet on a bleak moor.
They crouch in the shelter of a crumbling cairn and talk of the
heroes of their youth.*)

FIRST SHEPHERD:
Nay, Owain was the brightest bard I knew!
Why, I've been sitting in the hall at dusk
When down the pathway of his golden voice
Princes and their ladies have, like trees
Graceful in blossom, danced a stately step;
When men, on horses whinneying in the wind,
Have galloped in the air above our heads;
And swine, exulting on a battlefield,
Have made the darkness horrible with shrieks
From some poor wretch whose rest their tusks have tricked
Back into life, when all they prayed was death!
I have been there when . . .

SECOND SHEPHERD:
                    Rightly is thy name
Will of the Wagging Lip! Why, I would speak
Of Brian, maker of more mourners than
The ten-mouthed dragon under Caradoc!
Not one day since it left the Humped One's forge

Has his long blade been dry of fellow's blood!
He'd say, the West wind wrinkling his black beard,
'Dickon,' that's me, 'if once this edge were dry
Why, this old sexton's friend would crack in bits,
And what would Parson do then, if you please!'
A bonny killer, boys! I've known him when
No enemy was left, to burn his neighbour's thatch
And stick his board-friends as they stumbled out!
His very hounds one day made food for hawk,
And all because he was too tired to hunt!
A bonny killer, yes! Why, hill-talk says,
His own old mother . . .

THIRD SHEPHERD:
                    Stop, that is enough!
Between the two of you I smell the bones
That sway ten fathoms deep out in the Sound!
These lads you boast of stand as high as dogs
Against our Michael of the Fishing Boats.
Ah, what a darling of a man, and more
Than seven feet high, I lay my oath to that,
Arms like a pine-trunk and a lion's head!
Why, when he took to sea on Summer morns
Even the mermen called out to their wives
To lie within the caves until his keel
Had passed! And his trim craft was hardly known
To sail beyond the shadow of the Craig
Unless its wake was thick with lusting seals;
Queens every one of them, jealous for the night
When the smooth pelts would slip from milky sides
And let them dance like wantons by the shore;
Each burning for the touch of Michael's hand,
He floating in the froth of their hot blood!

FIRST SHEPHERD:
No, I will not hear another word
Of blasphemy like this. Have senses left
Your skulls that this maid's talk should tumble out
Like scum upon the babbling pot of broth?

THIRD SHEPHERD:
A canny fisher, Michael lad! A boy!

FIRST SHEPHERD:
A whoremonger, my man, no match for bard!

SECOND SHEPHERD:
But oh the bonny killer, Brian bach!

THIRD SHEPHERD:
Quiet, I hear a lamb lost by the Llyn.

FIRST SHEPHERD:
Let's hurry. I can smell the thunder's voice!

SECOND SHEPHERD:
The finest killer man has ever seen!

XII

O, where they came from with their coloured songs
Only the sea-bird and the seal might say;
Why they should tease the incorrigible sea
It is known alone to blood, and theirs is shed.

What we do know is stuff enough for dreams
And little more; joy in the dancing blade,
And love, no ecstasy, as the bright word soared. . . .
Then they were followed by a darker race.

So red brands leapt around them as they went
From the red lowlands to the redder West;
And as they knelt for mercy from the sea
They heard their dragon dying in the hills.

A tongue they carried, and a trick with truth,
And songs to make God's very angels weep;
And straight they held their gallant golden heads
And walked in woods where burning green eyes watched.

They took with them proud memory of a king,
And dying, one by one, forgot their names;
A race of singers walked into the mist
And left their bones to whiten on the crags.

What did they leave? A fantasy of stone,
And seven old women singing at the nets,
A half-forgotten festival of song,
And a blue-eyed boy who watches for the boats.

XIII
EVACUATION FROM THE ISLES

And so the boats called, and the Isles were bereft
Of men, women, nets and sheep;
All goods to the mainland where living is cheap.
Only the unprofitable dogs were left.

Now, when the black cloud probes the island sky,
These lost ones stand
In obedient terror, or pacing lonely sand,
Look up expectant at the curlew's cry.

For something is gone that the tall gods gave;
The echo of words
Only now in the wind and the mocking sea-birds.
Ahead, the impassable wave.

THE SHADOWS OF MY WORDS

The shadows of my words hold fast my hands;
'Bring no more ghosts to join us,' say their tears.
'Start no more musics in the air. O leave
The sultry wind to sing its own despair.'

The spirits of my acts walk round the home,
Nod as I nod my head before the glass;
'Lie still,' they say, 'and let the world wag on:
Lie in your bed and tell the future's beads.'

I watch tomorrow wear away the moon;
I count time's slow erosion of my hopes.
Can it be then that Master Hand, Sir Tongue,
Were never more than moment's ragged apes?

FUGITIVE

As one who walks in dusty courts
Or in forgotten palaces,
Tapping the wainscot with a shaking hand,
Avoiding mirrors, listening for the Lord;

As one who, riding from his fear,
Wakes in the land of dreams to find
His earth-old enemy inside the room,
Offering a hand that smells of church-yard loam;

Or one who, when the merry pipe
Restores the grass to highways, sees
Approaching in the grinning shape of hate
The very creature that his knife had nulled;

So tread I on the rim of death
With lute to cover lack of sword,
With robe where iron should be worn,
And heart a-flutter at the plover's word!

THE POSSESSORS

The tyrant who keeps court within my hand
Tears up the promise of the morning word.
Poor bird, locked in a doorless cage, and blind;
Poor hand, so needing love, so made to slay!

The courtly fool who dallies on my tongue
Smells battles in the air, and would be clothed
In iron harder than the Winter's ice.
Brave as a warrior, he wags his bells!

So these fine two strut up and down my days,
One with his hawk, the other with a lute,
Bowing each-other in and out of rooms
That give upon the avenues to death,
Erasing public pose in secret acts;
One hawks for love — the lutanist plucks hate!

POEM

The pod bursts open and the seed
Is left for all to see;
So from the mouth breaks forth the word
To all eternity.

The fire that flares upon the hill
Is soon too fierce to hide,
Nor can man now undo the spell
That festers in the word.

Once uttered, sound falls like a germ
Into the womb of life,
To ferment and at last to form
The progeny of grief.

If only love grew through the eyes,
And hate sprang from the hands,
With word we could paint Paradise
A solitude of sounds.

If only grief lay in a shroud,
And fear danced on a sword,
We could turn back the scarlet tide,
Strike free the trembling word!

VARIED GROWING

The body grows as brick on brick
Builds high the mansion made by man;
But spirit comes to plentitude
As note on note creates a tune.

Leaf from leaf makes known a tree,
As birch by beech gives name to wood;
But what the limits of delight?
And which the worlds within a word?

Before the tongue falls back to rest
Another lie has angered God;
Even the sword maintaining peace
Rusts quietly in last year's blood.

The hand that carves for man's increase
Of pleasure spoils the graceful stone,
Or showing truth in child of love
Turns back to find a faceless bone!

THREE STEPS FOR A POET

A little lad along the lane
Has told the hedgehog all his pain,
And on the downs at dead of night
Has called to curlew in his fright.

The smiling man with shining eyes
Has made his songs with lovely lies.
He sold his birthright for a groat
To learn the language of the stoat.

The old magician, cold as clay,
Sits at his simples night and day,
Rehearsing his address to God,
At their close meeting under sod.

THE BARRIERS

Between the muscle and the hammer-head,
The liquor and the veinous leaf it feeds;
Between the vision and the throne of God,
The promise and the stillborn shrouded words;

Between the hope that flies, the fear that dives,
The beak of hawk, the pretty breast of wren;
Between the husk that dries, the seed that thrives,
The line that flames, and that which leaves the pen,

Stand blood, its channel and the broken cross,
The bed unslept-in and the worn-down shoe,
The fruit of pity and the breast of Christ,
And all the bones kissed clean beneath the sea.

And would you say it even if you could,
Smash cage and let the weary words fly free?
Might that not let the tiger from the wood,
And madness ride across the morning sky?

THERE IS A CAUSE FOR FAITH . . .

There is a cause for faith, if also one for fear,
In the magnificently open hate of tiger:
The bull roars and lacerates the earth,
And by that sign we know nobility
Of purpose, less infirm than midnight knife,
Or governmental salve before guns growl.
All things unmade by men, fresh from the fist
Of God without our aid, walk in the light;
The stoat's quick victory, the feats of fox,
And bat's incredibly fine trapeze,

All, all are perfect in the eye of Heaven.
Only would I wish to be set free
From the bead-bright eyes, the surreptitious nudge,
And the twittered malice of the watching birds!

THE VARIED FACES

With beak and skull the laughing mummers come,
Hands in their sleeves and pennies on their eyes,
Bawling a ballad to the empty room,
Led by the wicked, followed by the wise.

Brave first kills dragons with a wooden sword,
Sweet second rides to knowledge on a snail,
Dumb third sings love-songs to a dangling bird,
But fourth inscribes Christ's story with a nail

Upon the flint that one day from a bow
Will leap, as arrow-head, into Man's heart,
Bringing the message and laying Satan low.
So Man will come to Heaven in a cart.

I did not think so many varied faces
Moved in the world, or held such varied places.

CHRIST CHILD

Warm as a little mouse he lay,
Hay kept him from the Winter's harm;
Bleating of puzzled lamb he heard,
And voices from the near-by farm.

His mother's eyes were bent on him
As to her frozen breast he clung;
His father stopped the draughty cracks
And sang a merry herding song.

Who would have thought upon that hour
Those little hands might stay a plague,
Those eyes would quell a multitude,
That voice would still a rising wave?

Only the omens of the night,
The lowing ox, the moaning tree,
Hinted the cruelty to come:
A raven croaked, 'Gethsemane!'

BETRAYAL

I cast the dice and lusting one came up;
My hours of joy were snatched across the board.
I watched the grey hand with its talons creep
Into my childhood, deadly as a sword.
The bone box rattled, fell the grinning cube
And showed upon its side the lying two.
My present, like a dove within my robe,
Fluttered and gave itself to grasping woe.

So once again I shook, and watched the seven
With fearful eyes. I heard the dark shape speak;
'This is an entertainment fit for Heaven;
Finer than rack or stake, or blinding beak!'

And then he took the cup and flung a three.
A thief was hanging either side of me.

SECOND COMING

I
RESURRECTION

The days moved slowly with a sick-room breath;
And then at midnight the great stone rolled.
Who saw the tortured spirit cross the heath
Like crackling leaf when Autumn wind blows wild?
Not the poor soldier sodden with cheap wine,
The helmet callous thick upon his chin;
Nor the sick beggar coughing in the rain,
Opening his rags to let cold bounty in.

Who heard in the air the dead man's wail,
The scream of triumph from the man just born?
Perhaps the milkmaid scrubbing at her pail,
Or the young nun, her gold hair newly shorn.
But no-one shuddered as the spirit passed;
One night's enough for such white pain to last.

II
THE NEW WAY

A beggar ran in flapping rags
And shod in broken shoon;
The village dogs sniffed at his legs
And horror howled at the moon.

A lady sat among her hounds,
Dressed in a silken gown;
Can comfort salve your wounded hands,
And love your eyes of pain?

The beggar and the lady white
Sat at the self-same board,
And ere next day had grown to night
They lay as wife and lord.

Oh beggar where is your ragged coat,
Oh where your shoes so worn?
All that has died as dies the night
Before the merry morn.

Oh beggar leave your silken bed
And come to us from your bower.
I'll come to the world in my own good time,
But with a Prince's power!

III
THE SEASONAL MIND

There are dark seasons of the mind where grow
The fruits of terror and the crops of woe, where fly
Strange birds whose sombre songs like death-knells ring
Through the soul's woods, where no dawn-bird dare sing.

There are black transmutations of the heart
That change caresses into festering hurt,
Turning the Prophet with his peaceful beard
To roaring bearer of the flaming sword.

Who knows the magic of an ermine cloak,
Heart's royal disguise, although the heart should break?
The cross can make a body meat for worms,
Or turn a prayer to mindless, whimpering moans.

But lips and cloth-of-gold can make a King
Of what was left a dangling lifeless thing.

IV

THE SERMON IN THE FIELD

The Prince walked out in purple,
He galloped out in gold,
To speak with all the people
That stood in Judas' field.

His black hair hung in ringlets
All bound with silver bands,
And gay hawks shod with opals
Stood on his jewelled hands.

The people heard his gospels,
They wept to hear his songs,
And watched the pattern woven
By sunlight on his rings.

Until a child's voice shattered
The magic by a word,
'Look! Underneath his golden coat
There's blood upon his side!'

And as the words were spoken
A cock began to crow,
And from the village stables
We heard the oxen low.

They tore off all the purple,
They quarrelled for the gold,
And left the gay hawks broken
And dying in the field.

V
SECOND CRUCIFIXION

Time lay like a stone upon the hill;
Birds fell through thick black air, nigh glad
So soon to die. Struck blind, the tottering sun
Tapped his slow way behind the echoing cloud.

We shuddered in the valley as a wail
Rose from the crowd about the cross, and stared
At the twitching white thing that had been
A Prince in purple till the cock had crowed.

What centuries of suffering we have seen
Waiting this moment. . . . Now the Prince has passed
Again, and still we bear the same old pain.
Oh shall we never rest, not till the last?

We left this madness, stumbling back afraid,
To find the child still sobbing in the field.

VI
A THIEF TO HIS LORD

Holy Jack, they say your side bled gold;
They say flame leapt from holes across your brow.
And Jack, that flowers sprouted from your hands
Where iron drove them hard against the bough.

I wish I had been there, old lad of love;
You must have looked a king upon that tree!
I'm game to wager either of my ears
The guards looked small against your majesty.

I met a woman in the tavern here
Who says they wept, the folk, to hear you jest
At being given wine upon a sponge.
And did you then? I always miss the best!

Oh, Jack, don't hold it hard against me that
I stabbed a soldier later for your coat.

VII

A Young Nun to her Lover

Oh Lord, the blood that's crusted to your side
Is frozen love. Step down from that gaunt tree
And let my passion warm you, who, afraid
Of mortal union, nightly long to be
Christ's blushing bride. I swear I could not dread
Caresses from those mutilated hands;

Ah, should your broken fingers weave a braid
Of my gold hair, I'd wrap the golden bands
About that shrunken throat to keep you close;
Always my love; bereft of you, no peace.
I walk in winter though my years spell Spring,
My lips on fire for your hallowing.

Can you not come again, my love, and know
This gold before it turns white as the snow?

LOVE POEM

Let us go out in the rain, love,
And keep these memories clean;
Then stand beneath the sheltering eave
To fall in love with the moon.

And let us walk in the wood, dear,
Walk in the stillness of pines,
And sigh for the wild birds who cry there
All night in their shuddering dreams.

Then back to our waiting house, sweet,
Four walls and a sturdy roof,
Where nothing can ever harm us —
No, not even grinning Death.

LOVE SONG

Distance nor death shall part us, dear,
Nor yet the traitor word;
And love shall live within our home
As blithe as any bird.

The sight of you is in my eyes,
Your touch is in my hand;
They cannot part us now, my love,
With miles of weary land.

Man with his sword and Death his scythe,
Are but the tricks of time,
To tease me with the empty years
Before we shared one name.

110

TEARS ARE TOO SMALL

Tears are too small a sign of grief,
My love, oh my sweet love!
A child will cry himself to sleep
As though his golden heart would break,
And yet will laugh himself awake
To see the morning cony leap.

Grief is too great to break a heart,
My sweet, though pain is there;
Too great for anything but death,
Blank madness underneath great seas,
Christ screaming from a million trees,
You, stark beneath a burial-cloth.

OH CHILD

Oh child, oh child,
From the leaves of night
Throw down a thought to suffering men,
From the silver boughs where rest your feet,
A pearly plum, a tear of love.

Oh child, my child,
The axe they whet
Will cut the love and kill the brain,
And sap will flow like a rain of jet,
Black dreams of knives hid in the sleeve.

Oh child, our child,
Break down the gate,
Burst through the undergrowth of pain
And come before it is too late,
Before we grow too grey to love.

DUMB LOVE

How do I love you then?
Till stone unfold his nature, and
Funereal rook his language,
Tongue dumb as bell unclappered
Lies in silent head.

How tell you hurt, my own?
Only as trees wind-anguished bend
And sigh their mournful message,
Or woman freshly widowed
Whispers to her dead.

How can it end, sweet Queen?
Only as leaf ends in the wind,
Blown to a new world's edge
For future's growth the food,
Rich as a dying word.

REVENANTE

The bells of memory sound this summer day
Down the long alleys of the blue-skied years;
Shy cowslip, thyme, the haunting scent of hay,
Pleached gardens nourished by a lover's tears,
And honeysuckle, shy maid in the hedge,
Are all Her handmaids; blessed is the sight
The mirror-pool caught of Her. So the stage
Is set for entrance, and a girl in white
Walks in my heart again, out of pale death,
Kingdom of shrivelled mouth and powdering bone,
Touching my cheek with flower-laden breath,
And whispering, 'Poor love, and still alone?'
Was any man so lucky, dear God?
It will be dawn before She takes the road.

CAPTURED MOMENT

Now creeps the weary blood his way
Through body's ruined lanes,
Sacked by a decade's history
And crucified to victory,
House of a thousand pains.

Now hang the threadbare thoughts upon
The mind's fire-blackened bough,
No longer green or gold, as when
That early Spring bade, 'Spring again,
O Youth, life is for you.'

Then minnow-minutes flashed so fast
That years ran like a day,
Though sun in fleetness never passed
The window where love died at last,
And skull put on its clay.

THE DILEMMAS

Through the dark curtain of desire
Leaps the white avenging sword,
Passion's assassin, as blood in a fire
Blossoms as accusing word.

Should deed be done, or thought be dared,
The uncaged fury of the heart
Like subtly exquisite bird
Would blood his beak ere scream could start.

Yet should the book be left unread,
The door unlatched, who'd dare defy
And face from sterile unshared bed
The future's pale unblinking eye?

LOVE SONNET

These fleshy capes and bays uncharted be,
For fickle seasons of the soul deny
Facility for sounding. Glance away —
The transmutation's over! You shall see
Another terrain that shall tease your eye,
New beacons lighting routes to other dreams.
And scarcely anything is what it seems
In this enchanted garden. Do but sigh,
And from the bronze pagodas in her breast
Come sounds of passion's piety. Now laugh,
And love's sweet harlotry begins to scoff,
Tender as wren upon her ruined nest.
But since this voyage costs me more than life,
Come, come, my love, you shall not put me off!

OPHELIA

The frail girl floating with the stream
Saw life to be a sea-green dream

Of flitting ghosts she once had feared
Who stroked her face and disappeared.

She watched the old man fast asleep
And saw the muttering figure creep

Away with poison-horn in hand;
But this she could not understand.

She saw the curtain move, and heard
The scream that started as a word.

She watched the Queen fill up the bowl
To barter two crowns for a soul,

And while the Players spoke their words
She saw the old King dreaming swords.

She watched the pale boy kiss a bone
And knew then that his love was gone,

And opened her clenched hand to see
The button that let madness free.

And so her wound began to flower;
Her head was crowned with blossom-shower.

Swift carp caressed her quiet breast
And linnets carolled from the nest.

She called to conies on the bank
And smiled, and sighed, and slowly sank.

And from his bough the squirrel said,
'There's no more weeping when you're dead.'

SAD SONG

O black the wind and salt the tear
And sad the lonely curlew's call;
O grey the unattended fire,
And grey the watchers in the hall.

He too was once a laughing lad
Whose hair was fickle in the wind,
Until fear crept into his bed
And dulled the edges of his mind.

And she, a Princess in her bower,
Of all world's treasures his alone,
Until she saw death in a flower
And woke to find her heart had gone.

O bleak the wind and cold the fire,
And still the summer peewit's call:
Two wanderers sit as night draws near
And stare across the empty hall.

THE BALLAD OF THE PRINCE

PROLOGUE

'Soe one shal come in the yeares when I am gone, with raven's cloke and eye of the hawke.

Heare ye the wordes that he shal speke, wych shal bee of a Prince that is the Christ, and a King that is the evill Godde of Oppression.

Heere shal bee Darkness of the Pit and no Light; the Sepulchre but no Flowers; the Serpent but no manner of Delight. By Treacherie shal the Savyour bee slayne and the People know Usurie and Paine at the handes of them that sit in Unrighteousnesse. Thys is the World in a Glasse, as it shal bee when men know not the Prince of Peace, forswering Loving-kindnesse for the sake of Riches, and Wisdom in their ruling for the Sworde.'

(*The World in a Glasse*. Anon. 1612.)

I

THE BALLAD OF THE PRINCE

I prick a poem with an adder's tongue
Across the parchment of the living ram:
Where gibbet's minions in the midnight swing,
Wrapped in my wolf's warm wool I dream my dream.
For I am more than mankind; my hungry eye
Equals, swears yokel, falcon's screaming fate,
And when my hair is lash across the air
Old shapes come mopping to me from the wheat
That thrusts thin craven hands from Judas' field,
Craving a bounty from the matron clouds
Whose promise is a pitcher, kindly-round,
Which pours in tilting nothing but bright words.
What I shall tell you stands, though men should come
To drive nails through my hands and break my home.

II

HIS COMING AND THE FEAR

Proud as an ancient prayer-wheel, the Prince
Stepped with a purple flutter from the tomb,
Kissing the silver locks, the carven ghoul
That with a dead-sea majesty untwined
His dappled-days to come from hers now spent.
She, cut in monumental marble, lay,
Long limbs arranged, and only the gold fillets
Of her hair alive, twinkling like brazen eyes
From dusty archives of a temple cell
On ancient hills, where kings rode on a cloud
With trees for slaves, nourished on lightnings.

117

Fanfare from convolvulus, drum the poppy's pod,
His majesty predicted. Over lawns
Prim peacocks' grating called him back to men.

Curls in the candle magic from the caves
Where Merlin masked the goat with royal grace:
Burnished, the bright brands cluster; bannered eaves
Bell my lord's majesty, that when he rise
From off the three-legged stool of humbleness
His vassals vow the Christ has come again,
For all the holy emblems that the eyes
Bequeath about the palace yard. Rain
Like holy liquor kisses calloused lips
That in the drought had relished mouldering roots
Stored for their swine. Bright linnets on the paps
Of Margery and Moll fan tiny heats
Of reverence towards the Prince, whose hand
Proclaims a feast across the suffering land.

'Come with the banner. Come with the bugle-horn.
Break as the frost cracks flax the spell that binds
My lilied hankerings within this room.
See, worlds below this window, cypress bends,
Nods like that withered crone upon the wall
Whose eyes have watched me since I was a child.
'It shall be pestilence,' the boughs' mouths wail,
'See how the linnets topple!' I am afraid
That night's donation to my peace will be
The lurching leper crouching by my door,
The black old priest whose fingers leap with glee
Upon the sleeping breast, whose long teeth gnaw
Red tunnels to the fount-head of the heart,
To suck the summer-dreams that did no hurt.

Let me talk with the oak and the swinging bird,
Know the slow suffering of prisoned roots;
In the straw-dry throat and brittle beak,
Taste the black leaden bubble of despair.

When deafening shadows creep across the earth,
And death walks like a lady through the streets,
I watch the poison-ivy through a crack
Thrust a thin finger in my future's ear.
Wail with the willow, love the whistling lark:
Beneath the leaf the starved snail craves our tears.
Take snake for brother, fondle the swift hawk,
By whelping vixen spend the cobweb hours.
For we are what the world is; words and talk
Blow through us, blunt as a blind boy's eyes.

In the belly of the bud on a branch of iron,
Deep in the granite forest of my fear,
Beats, fragile as a prisoned linnet's hopes,
A pulse no fiercer than a half-thought word.
Through veins as narrow as the fairy throat
Of fancy's humming-birds among the vines,
Sweeps, with a minute majesty, the flood
Whose microscopic melody is heard by none
Save those who nightly journey over motes
From the far poles of suffering and delight;
Who know the silver whistles of the wind
That shriek like thunder from the flower's bell.
And what shall this bud bear in later dreams,
A pear of pleasure, or a bough for Christ?'

III
THE WIZARD'S DAUGHTER

The girl in the spendthrift habit of despair,
Dyed in the wailing anthem of Christ's blood,
Festoons the foliage of her hair and sings;
The bright-minted music of her throat
Swims through the world of less-than-yesterday,

Probes the forgotten limits of dismay,
That all the jewel-feathered denizens of cloud
From their brief cardboard parliament of green
Thrash upward, bursting like an Easter dream
Across the crystal leaves that tinkle tunes
Torn from the very magic of that sky
Which reddened with the Christ-child's blood, before
Heaven, even, ran to the rattling lock
That heralded disaster from a nail.

Mary she moves, with more than Mary-grace,
Among the grey unleavened progeny of stone,
Past the slow vastness of the sodden byre.
The ancient word that festers in her heart
Wails like a wasp and stirs her blood to song.
(Draw on the gilded glove of expectation!)
The frail acanthus budding from her lips
Blossoms with frothy promise of the day
When the pale spine-crowned prince upon his chair,
Warden of godliness, lord of the stricken lark,
Leans forward like the old man in the park,
And with a comely finger, shorn of fear,
Cozens her wayward blushes: the sweet hand
Strokes comfort where the cancer was to spring.

So through a summer, reckless in their ruin,
These two, the fustian-maid, her boy of gold,
Walked in the woods, ran laughing through the rain
Abreast, blest and forgot the wicked world.
And when the moths wove music through the dusk,
These two, hairs' strands entwined, lay in a bed
Of musk and tenderness, nor recked no risk.
But when the rigid leaves put on their red,
Meet courtiers for the king below the mould,
The old king's hornéd hand tricked up a spell,
For fear the brazen boy should glean his gold,
The lass strike free his servants. For their ill

Black runes he mustered, mastered with his eye
The dragging toad and his dark family.

The loom of fancy locks the coloured cord
In thousand arabesques. Under the hand
Writhe patterns that no stumbling poet's word
Can coax, like lark, inside a cage; or bind,
Crown of a rhymed delight in a maiden's hair
As she steals forward at the chosen hour.
From caul to shrouding cell full is the air
Of twangling instruments and tongues of fire
That twine and flourish in my body's house
Until its rooms rock, reek with unknown tales
Of old dark days, and men whose ardours fuse
Now with the probing vetch, dishonoured by the snails
Whose figuring slime itself a pattern curls
Around the world, where men are mankind's fools.

There did a lad forget his salt-eyed lass
And paced the lanes in converse with a twig.
There did a maid put on a gipsy-face
To sing grey songs along the stream, big
With no bairn but progeny of grief, full
Of no fancy but a fancy's child. Come dark,
And shepherd, vigilant upon the hill,
Shapes a quick talisman with crow-dropped stick
To fend his flock from evil, as her tale
Riding the wind, twists knife inside his veins.
Thus did the spell kill love and passion pale,
The old king chuckle, mumbling his runes
Among his black familiars, peopling the air
With leathern wings and voices red as fire.

That night the black-robed stranger tapped the pane
And heaven died. Deep in the caverns heart held
Shrank a dove, the strings of her dream aloud
Shouted for succour. It was a winter's night

And lanes beneath the grey hills whispered feet,
Feet treading worlds away to other worlds,
Legs forcing feet towards the weeping sea:
And her feet safe upon the hearth, away
From hills and sea and the winter lanes. Safe
From the terrors she had dreamed, that crouched like men
Masked by the trees, listening for feet:
Safe from the dwarf who lurched along the shore,
Here in her safe stone house she was secure
From all but the dark stranger at the door.

Cooler than winter's homage, passionate as pain,
Brighter than the unfurled flag of rose,
The gold-strings of the maiden's fancy twang
Music and madness, love, life and loss,
And a pauper prince in exile by the lake.
Through the cloak of the twilight his hair's soft strands
Circle her hands, like wished-for golden bonds
That chain her to dead dreams for the rest of her years,
In a world where the word is more strong than the thing,
Where the thing is a thought in a dead man's head.
Warmer than winter's homage, passionate as rain,
Whiter than the unsmirched lily-flower,
Is the broken cup, the body without bread,
Hands of the wrinkled woman in the barn.

(We watched, and from her mouth a black rose sprang, spreading
a churchyard fragrance through the room. Then knew we alabaster hands familiar with the wedding-place of seals, with leper's
hopes. The long, sick twilight tottered through the pane, and overhead we heard the cripple cough.

It was Sunday and along the damp road we knew young men and
women would be building homes.

The music in the dusk closed like a flower's bell, slowly, without
impediment, and we saw then that this old woman in her shawl

had moved in marble palaces, where sea had crept unhampered to
the very steps, drowning the white does and the merry clown, who
in another day would have brought word of peacock's feathers
floating on the waves, and the golden girl locked screaming in the
tower.)

IV
THE PRINCE PASSES

'I who have with these hands dug love a grave
A thousand times, in whose mad dreams of fame
Hope, like blind villain in a play, taps past
My gap-mouthed door, dragging his padded feet
Along the street, I and my word are alone.
Only my drunken room, whose windows leer
At other windows where another waits
For other love and other hope, my room
Knows something of the twisting worm that crawls
Between my midnight sheets rehearsing death,
Or halts upon my very lips as I,
Reprieving this live graveyard for a day,
Break bread, which had been happy in the breeze
Before the sharp scythe flickered, like my fears.

Brave as a wedding-ring, the brass-voiced clock
People's my private eye with dusty ghosts:
"Remember, Prince! Recall that tale of tears
You spun, eye cocked on the door, the day
You thrust a fist of barbs into her heart?"
Stern as sentinel-centaur the chorus clacks:
"Lilies and convovulus and bright-breasted rose
Bower-maidens acted around her bridal bed.
Know, man, they seemed to shudder as you pressed
Your princely lips upon her plain deal board,

And hours afterwards your wondering eyes
Were shackled to the thorn-print in your hand."
Brave as a wedding-ring — Oh, not that word!
Would it murder if I stabbed the clock?'

(Out of a clamour of swords, words' tatters tumble,
Like promises from youth upon a festival;
Curt as an adder, slim as a harp-string, nimble
As the sweating jester in the hall.
Under the worm-holed roof-tree elder's hands
Caress the licking tongues that blood craves now,
Content that one clear summer safely stands
Between their migrained harvest and the snow.
Along the geometric lawns red retinue
Of silken competence and flutes sails fair:
Wine flows as potent and smooth words as true
As was in any year before sharp war.
And the old king still, in bloody house of stone,
Scuffs gold into the coffer, clothed in iron.)

Swung from the ropes of his father's cackled rhyme,
Flung upward with a myriad scaléd things,
This sobbing saviour, tricked of heart and home,
Clove the wax clouds with wizard-borrowed wings.
Now, years below, the plum that was his globe
He saw, in silence dropping from God's tree;
The graceful galleon that walks upon the wave
Seemed like a drunk man's fancy, or a lie,
And all men's acts fantastic as a dream.
Far, far above he heard a trumpet speak
His Coming. Thunder, the celestial drum,
Dwindled that silver herald to a shriek
Such as the frightened mole speaks when the spade
Encroaches on his life; so shrieked the lad:

'Lack-facile, with finger of oil, the King,
Gleaner of heart-gourds, snaps the short grain

Of the flower of my faith, that the cream sap spurts
Constellation of verses, vaulting in rhyme
The unscaled tabernacles of the sky,
Over the sun-spot barriers of Heaven,
Where, pale as ivory petals in the dusk,
The maidens of the moon sing songs of mist,
Of red-veined warrior whose heart of steel
Shall lead him to their bowers of ecstasy,
Before the dawn unlocks the shackled door;
Before the dirge of children, chants of delight,
Bring hero candle to light him to his grave,
And spade of gold to keep the wolf away.'

He fell, and as he fluttered like a leaf
A century above the topmost crags,
He watched the story of his neighbour's life
Enact itself. He saw the million tricks
Held in his royal adversary's hand,
And knew himself for Joker. Down he fell
Until the contours of his promised land
Grew wider than his vision. Windy wail
Rose round about him from the mountain pines.
Pain in his head burst sudden like a pod,
Wrapped round his heart as vetch round pear-tree twines,
So that he knew himself at last for no true god,
And screamed with horror, as his body broke
One inch ere end, in dream, upon a stake.

V

A Courtier Speaks

'Lord, you have plucked their fruit: let them begone,
The rag-tag beggers who have kissed your hem.
Stay the black angel from their squealing swine
Lest famine halt before the groaning realm,

Lest years yet warmly wrinkled in the bud
No bright blades burgeon when you ride to war.
Step softly, lord, the priests are in their bed:
Break not the anthem that their stone hearts hear,
Or hard it surely shall go with us when
They know the silent sufferer on the tree
Was our devising, so that by the moon
Hill sketched a pleasing pattern of the three,
A prophet and two rogues. We let them swing,
That in our halls wine-heated harp should twang.'

VI

THE SHEPHERD LAD'S LAMENT

'I wake and know the day is not for me.
Under the tongue is tied a grain of sand
That snaps my appetite as I snap bread
Alone in the home. This is my hand
That stumbles like a stranger on the board;
My tired feet that dream of nursery boots
To twitch them seven long leagues away from me
And all my foolish frenzies. Oh my heart,
Stay with me now to help my head
Dictate a posture to this froward flesh
That knows no hate, no love but bread and wine;
This walking graveyard which, it is my fear,
Will one night in its sleepless bed lose faith,
And crack head, heart and hope all in one breath.

Brief months ago I loved a merry girl,
Whose fingers wove with mine a merry game.
While our flocks mingled, mingled was our tale
Of faith, and fullness and the fire-lit home.
Long days were dwarfed, quicksilvered by our glee,

The swallow taught our love the way to dance,
We learned from lambing-time the way to pray.
Yet that was years ago. Yes, that was Once
Upon a Time, when time was very young,
When I would leap broad rivers in my pride,
For longest mile was not a hand-breadth long,
And a laughing lass strode golden at my side.
Since then the doves have withered in their cote,
And gale-griped elms have shown their wrinkled root.

I know that time is like an eagle's wing;
Poised or impetuous it is the same
Inevitable thrust, harsh as a nail,
Grey as the old king's beard. The grave
Gives one solace at least; lodging it is
Where traveller may lie and count the hairs
Upon his head, by permutation find
What centuries are bound to linnet's breast.
Along the city's streets millennium of feet
Have acted chorus to uncounted words.
Along the lanes, all sparrows since the dawn
Of light have fluttered in among more leaves
Than lunatic holds dreams. Be still:
For only death grants time to count all time.

The blank page tells me no bright hero's name,
Nor does the face I see upon the wall.
My eyes a thousand times today have probed
Beneath the cloth, the leather and the steel
To lance the creeping tumour of my doubt.
Whose voice is that I hear among the trees?
Whose is the step that loiters on the stair?
This hand that holds out friendship or a blade,
Is it my brother's or a devil's? No,
My tongue's a fool and brain's a dupe to words!
Let heart be mistress, mouth shall only tell
The things she utters. What shall be the tale?

"Forget there was a difference. Take you his hand
For yours. Take then his feature. He is your shade!"'

Move with the wide moon and the wrinkling wind
That flicks old Abram's lyric like a whip
Across the dynasties. So shall they find
Boys kinging castles on the farm-yard heap,
Or trollops grubbing truffles in the dusk;
An ancient weapon, a design, a shard,
An old desire, a fractured name. Oh ask
Of leisured leaf a metaphor, one word
To clamp the stony wraith upon the sky
For every man to mimic. Make men a name
For far-gotten sin. Identify
The hate that from the archives hauled a shame
Upon the gilded heads that held no care,
Who, guilty of no good, forgot guilt's fear.

'The sea makes nightly dirges round my head.
There was a lady dressed in silk who strode
Magnificent, a Mary, through my blood.
Bright moths, the treasure of my heart, abode
Within her chamber, bringing her desires
As I lay ravished, to my hanging door.
The threadbare summer passed, flared autumn fires,
And when the snowman came she came no more.
I walked alone among the blazing sands,
Forgetting men: I raved upon a hill
To scratch the sun from Heaven with my hands.
But one day as I drank, the forest pool
Painted her picture rotten in his bed:
Then knew I how gods could undo a God!'

EPILOGUE

White haired, they tread upon tomorrow's edge,
The Prince, his maid, the poor cracked shepherd lad,

128

Already ghosts, making my rhyme their refuge
As I sit by the road to beg my bread.
So from the fable break I off a crumb
To paint you man and monarch in their sin
And peasant in his fetters, staring; dumb
With a pitiful desire. Yet, in the fern,
Young lovers still shall dream of gilded years,
When lark will laugh them from their tumbled bed;
When rain will tell fertility, and not Chirst's tears
For all the lovely lads whose hopes are bled
White; whose hands may never build the home
Their dream has promised. May they forever dream!

BALLAD

Oh come, my joy, my soldier boy,
With your golden buttons, your scarlet coat,
Oh let me play with your twinkling sword
And sail away in your wonderful boat!

The soldier came and took the boy.
Together they marched the dusty roads.
Instead of war, they sang at Fairs,
And mended old chairs with river reeds.

The boy put on a little black patch
And learned to sing in a tearful note;
The soldier sold his twinkling sword
To buy a crutch and a jet-black flute.

And when the summer sun rode high
They laughed the length of the shining day;
But when the robin stood in the hedge
The little lad's courage drained away.

Oh soldier, my soldier, take me home
To the nut-brown cottage under the hill.
My mother is waiting, I'm certain sure;
She's far too old to draw at the well!

As snowflakes fell the boy spoke so,
For twenty years, ah twenty years;
But a look in the soldier's eyes said no,
And the roads of England were wet with tears.

One morning, waking on the moors,
The lad laughed loud at the corpse by his side.
He buried the soldier under a stone,
But kept the flute to soothe his pride.

The days dragged on and he came to a town,
Where he got a red jacket for chopping wood;
And meeting a madman by the way,
He bartered the flute for a twinkling sword.

And so he walked the width of the land
With a warlike air and a jaunty word,
Looking out for a likely lad,
With the head of a fool and the heart of a bard.

WAR POEM

Don't stand at night by the gate, love,
He will not come again,
And there are eyes that laugh to see
The flowering of a pain.

Do not lay him a place, dear,
For you will eat alone;
Nor put you on that pretty dress,
The need for that is gone.

Just go into your room, lass,
And make yourself a prayer,
For that will be your strength now,
This many and many a year.

TO CERTAIN LADIES, ON GOING TO THE WARS

Goodbye ladies, O ladies sweet, goodbye,
No more the gentle flowers,
Another life I'll try.
No more the scented evenings,
The tussels in the hay,
It's time that I was leaving
To live another way.

O, there'll be blood, my ladies
(And not all mine, I hope),
And damp beds under hedges
And washing without soap.
Black lice will bite the body
That knew your friendly limbs;
In barrack-blocks I'll envy
Your silken-sheeted rooms.

But goodbye ladies, O ladies don't complain,
It's time I learnt to shoot straight
Or fly an aeroplane.
So many lads I knew once
Are rotting under sods:
I owe them this one journey —
So farewell, pretty birds.

PRAYER IN TIME OF WAR

In whitest hour of pain the iron air
Turns back the edge of words like knives of hope.
Frail music from the mouth of mortal man
Fades in the interstellar space between
The eye that sees the wound, the heart that knows;
And oceanic splendours of delight
Shrink to a dewdrop on a pauper's lips.
The child of love creeps back into the womb.

Black Angel, come you down! Oh Purge of God,
By shroud of pestilence make pure the mind,
Strike dead the running panther of desire
That in despair the poem put on wings,
That letting out the viper from the veins
Man rock the mountain with his two bare hands!

POEM BEFORE THE END

They who dreamed in the storm were well aware
Of wind's sharp tooth,
The way frost gnawed the marrow from the bone,
So that the waker walking stumbled and fell dead,
And singer on the edge of song
Sighed and was dumb.

They who dreamed warm indoors arranged the flowers
Red against white,
Sin against chastity, chuckling at their joke:
Beautiful cowards, brave behind the lock,
They lay on silken couches, dead
Drunk with decay.

132

Yet both awoke to watch the same red dawn
Shriek from the hills,
To see the raven riding from the West
With love's white hand still bloody in his beak:
Yes, both sprang to their feet before
Freedom returned.

THE CONSCRIPTS

I

The sobbing stump of loss
Bled in his head;
And creeping crabwise through his heart
Despair dug out
The sockets of his hope, so that
He saw no sun,
Nor watched the cony at his trade
Among the mounds,
Nor tasted treasure in the wind
That blew from beds
Of peony and hyacinth,
Nor heard the quivering cadence high
Above his head,
The lark's gay coral necklet, meet
To move the dead,
Those very souls who lay wrapped
In the turf he trod,
Wise in their impotence, longing to leap
From their clay cells
To life, however harsh, brave pain
To see the sun!

133

II

I heard him weeping as the moon came up,
'Why must I suffer for a nation's lies?
My limbs lie bleeding on forgotten hills?
My dreams fall broken by the laugh of fools?'

I watched the patient cherry-tree lean down
To touch his waxen cheek. I heard her say,
'I suffer too, my love, but fruit will come
Though bird take blossom and man break down bough.'

III

They come, in the morning of glory, their wings to the sun,
Gallant and glistening, golden these lads of despair.
They ride in the wind, singing, their bright blood a screen,
Trailing, brave token of freedom, like flames in the air.

No more the tremulous pipe, the stuttering drum,
No more the cautious bolt, the empty bed;
But cymbals and the splendid trumpet's scream,
Greeting these glorious ghosts who stride from the dead,
Maimed but magnificent. They come, oh look, they come!

CONQUEROR

His words he banished like a worthless son
To walk upon the world without a name;
His songs he sharpened into darts, or thorns
To prick the thoughtless heart of happiness.
Alone,
He hunted where the mist flowed like a shroud.

When summer's plums proclaimed a festival
He fed on roots and berries, clothed in black,
His curses turned the milk of music sour,
And as he passed great houses fell to dust.
Alone,
He sought a mate with hands as strong as his.

And when the lark fell frozen from the air
He knew delight, knew laughter in a bone;
And when Hope's prayer lay festering on the lips
He laughed to see what wit there was in fear.
Alone,
Blowing the sun backwards into yesterday!

Come, he told the trembling dove, and lie
Against the furnace of my breast, be brave!
Though feathers fall, my love shall keep you warm;
You shall know tenderness and sup on tears!
Alone,
Next to his heart he wore an ounce of dust!

Stay, he told the weeping maid, and be
Pleasure for night-time in the mouldering straw!
I offer you the kingdom of despair,
And two sharp nails to decorate your hands!
Alone,
He spoke these love-words to the leaden pool.

So, through the world he carved, they went,
Man, a shadow and a tattered bird,
Until the seasons he invented lay
Behind them like forgotten promises.
Alone,
Walking the road towards an empty town.

MARTYR

He lay, wrapped in a world of mutilated hands,
Of trees that walked by night and grinning clouds;
To bellowing of bulls, his dream's black cloth
Ripped and let drop a heart stuck full of swords.

He walked, and by his side there strode a shade
Whose tattered hood half-hid a ram's dry skull:
'There is a place set for me at God's side.'
Said Ram, 'A door swings open outside Hell!'

He rose, upon hysteric wreaths of love,
Soared, nailed to an unrelenting beam;
Through airs that tingled with a child's low cries
He glided, gentle as a girl's soft dream

Of hyacinth and marjoram, in bowers
Of vernal holiness, where at a sigh
The leaves bend back like gracious hostesses
To introduce a lover, golden in glee.

He smashed the bowl of bitterness, let spill
His freighted nightmares on the weeping world.
His soul, ecstatic as the chains fell free,
Sped in the likeness of a tiny bird.

TO THE EDGE AND BACK

I

Sleep comes to Princes in their beds
And to the shepherd underneath a bush.

Sleep shuts the eyes of murderous owl
And gives tomorrow to the trembling wren;

Sleep dulls the edge of falling sword
And lets the song grow downward on the page;

Sleep tells the poisoned fungus swell
And blossom form upon the healing herb.

II

I fell asleep before my body's time
And made the endless journey along roads
No other foot had ever touched before,
Through lands no map could catch, or catching, hold;
Whose creatures had not burst on other eyes,
And whose elaboration no known tongue
Might tackle. Alone, without a stick I stepped.
Right to the edge of Nothing did I go,
Where no hope was, nor peace had ever been.
Back to the womb, back to a point in time
When womb itself was but an ecstasy
Of speculation in the atoms' swirl.
Back, back and back, until the word
Bloomed slowly as the sun across a plain.

III

In the beginning was the bird,
A spume of feathers on the face of time,
Man's model for destruction, God's defence.

Before man, a bird, a feather before time,
And music growing outward into space,
The feathered shears cutting dreams in air.

Before birds, a God, a Nothing with a shape
More horrible than mountains or the Plague,
A Voice as large as fate, a tongue of bronze.

Before this, O no before was there.
Where? Among the placeless atoms, mad
As tale the maggot makes locked in the skull.

And so I state a bird. For sanity
My brain's lips blow the tumbled plume.
I see it prophesy the path winds take.

IV

God on the edge of swords
Looked in man's heart and found distress,
Hands turned to Hell, and cut them off.

Man on the edge of God
Gazed in the furnace of desire
And turned to kneel before the Past.

Past on the edge of man
Pulled tight the rack, put back the clock,
And left a dream of twilight graves.

Man on the edge of Past
Admired the future, loved a bird,
And gazed into the eye of God.

V

Prophets, priests and kings
And the bell that rings
And the wolf that sings
And the snake that stings

Princes, knaves and witches
And the hand that twitches
And the ghoul that watches
And the scream of wretches

138

Boy, ghost and love
And the death above
And the frightened dove
And the poisoned glove

Come tear, purge, sack
Give take lose lack
Break bar and break the lock
And let the Babe be given back.

VI

The feet of Princes trammel
The wings of darkness,
Mothering multitudes of tears,
Blood from a stone.

Coloured the words and wings,
Joyful the golden lute,
Even the shy scabias
And the crumbled shell.

The sighs of madmen fatten
On the dead Knight's heart,
Tearing the wind like a sheet,
Cry 'God' beneath the sea.

VII

To One sleep comes as life,
Dressed in the song of birds and lit
By coloured lanterns of the heart,
Gay mummer mumbling of love and sunlit hills.

To Two life comes as dream
Before the mind's damp twigs flare out
And blossom as a furnace in the head;
Comes with a lie of half-forgotten Kings.

To Three sleep comes as dream,
The sand-dry scarecrow staring out
Above the city's roofs, dismayed
At sparrows' gossip on the chimney-tops.

To Four sleep comes as death,
Her garments tattered as a scream,
Failing to hide the bony steps
That tread from pleasure to the edge of doom.

VIII

Come, said the shrouded figure, taking my hands in his thin bones. An icy draught swept round us, through us, against us, driving our frozen bodies up the chill stone steps to the fire-blackened roof. Look, said my friend, and tell me what you see.

I see the fires of the future and the death of each day's life, I said, trembling with pride.

That it not enough, being merely one of rhetoric's outworn shoes, hissed the hooded memory. Look yet more closely and report your vision with accuracy, for, as you would see if you dared look, my eyes are but jungle-pools of fever-ridden mists swirling in the deep sockets; the eyes of the King of Darkness, of the Bard, of the Dead. They are not the reasonable cameras of ordinary men, but are starved of the common meat that even a pauper may command. So look again, man, and tell me what you see.

I stared across the city, terrified of failure, of the grinning figure at my side, and the knowledge sight would bring.

And my eyes, leaving the pestilence that raged inside my head, flew like two swallows in and out among the house-tops, along broad avenues and narrow alleys, over bridges and under triumphal arches, in at blistered doors and out at broken windows, above poplars and cottage apple-trees, chimney stacks and furnaces, the destinies and desires of half-a-million sufferers.

And, sick with horror, I heard my tongue awakening from its tomb of silence, heard the purple psalms that it was beginning to sing at the feathered bidding of its two capricious messengers.

And with the nails of my free hand I scratched the words I heard upon the harsh parapet where I stood; desirous not of perpetuation, nor of immortality and history, but only that these white-hot minutes should not sear away my spirit, leaving the body's nest a heap of ashes, to which no swallow might return upon the dawn. And as I wrote, the words appeared across the sky above my head in signs of fire, in all the colours of damnation, and attended by a distant singing, as of the Sad Ones from under the hill who find that the promised Paradise is one of stone and the eternal sobbing of the wind across a sunless moor.

And this is what I wrote across heaven:

> I see the half-born babe, unkindly formed,
> Screaming to be taken back from life.
>
> I see life slowly dripping from the bed
> Of the old man who cannot find his son.
>
> I see the boy examining his hand
> And praying God will clean away the sore.
>
> I see the mother holding close her child
> And kissing tight the staring, suffering eyes.
>
> I see the marriage-bed where lies no bride;
> The hand that never will hold victory;
>
> The knife that never will cut honest bread,
> The corpse of gladness propped against the door.

Then I heard the thunders of History, vast as the plains of solitude and horrible as gongs of brass; and all the pain that crawls on the face of worlds entered my side, traveling faster than light, along the fungoid channels of my blood, knocking like a conqueror at the portals of my head. Heart burst with anguish and sins more numerous than a pit of adders burst inside my body's cells. And each cell screamed aloud, swelling with sounds more terrible than Niagara's madhouse vision. And I fell. . . .

141

IX

I fell across the plains of Tartary,
The screaming hell of frozen flame and hate,
Where hooded figures walk in solitude

Across the glittering seasons whose bright plums
Cheat clutching fingers on the Lepers' Isle;
I wept to see the anguish in their eyes.

Across the hills where shaggy horsemen mass,
Thick as an anger, sniffing for the blood
That shall bring peace across the world's sick face.

Down avenues of memory, of time itself,
Back with the night-bird's cry unto the seed
Of starting, to the very feet of God.

And God there waiting in the shape of goat,
His dull eyes smiling, and the hanging lip
Tasting corruption from the midnight breeze;

The four sharp hooves tearing the page of truth,
The dead beard trembling with bloody worms
And passion quavering behind yellow teeth.

Back, back and down, until the body's voice
Shrank smaller than a grain of mustard-seed,
And fell and shrivelled and was blown away.

X

The morning cock
Shatters the crystals of sleep.
The fragments tinkle down
Into the dark pit I have left.

142

The screaming dies;
The many clutching hands
Fall backwards, down, down.
And morning air is clean and sweet.

I smell the hay,
The smoke of burning logs.
I hear the clanking churns,
The kitten crying at the door.

And so I learn
The kindness of the world,
The cock's assuring voice,
The safety in a bowl of flowers.

XI

There must be ways of locking the soul's door,
So that a man may sleep in peace at nights.

There must be prayers that keep the body safe,
Proof against the poison of a dream.

There must be songs to sing before sleep comes,
So that walls stand and seas may not be crossed,

There must be herbs to charm away the spot
I saw upon my hands when I awoke.

LYRIC

Oh keep your sweetness clover;
Days will come
When men no longer wish to feast on blood.
White May, Spring's bridal daughter,
It would be shame
To lose you from the battle-shattered wood.

And lilac, loveliest as I walk
At evening time
Along the road that brings me to my home,
I know if you could talk
Your words would be fit fellows for the strain
Of virginals, and Time

Would stay his shuffling feet,
Thin hand to ear,
And listen to your poems in the hedge.
And did I forget you, sweet
Poppies, as you rear
Those gallant scarlet heads, as red as rage?

I ask forgiveness then, whose heart is small
To house all beauties that delight my soul.

LINCOLNSHIRE BOMBER STATION

Across the road the homesick Romans made
The ground-mist thickens to a milky shroud;
Through flat, damp fields call sheep, mourning their dead
In cracked and timeless voices, unutterably sad,
Suffering for all the world, in Lincolnshire.

144

And I wonder how the Romans liked it here;
Flat fields, no sun, the muddy misty dawn,
And always, above all, the mad rain dripping down,
Rusting sword and helmet, wetting the feet
And soaking to the bone, down to the very heart. . . .

THE HEART'S WILD GEESE

Heart must always come again to home,
Like the wild geese who wheel their way through time
Back to the timeless pool and homely sedge.
They who went questing, screaming to the edge
Of man's small world, over the edge some say,
Have seen the iceberg's glory, seen the way
The coloured sun hangs curtains in the sky,
The barren coves where ancient whales still lie
Covered with barnacles as old as Spain,
Living the glorious bloody days again
When dragon-prowed boats first thrust through their dream.

All this the wild geese see, and their strange scream
Sounds back along the centuries. They know
Where palaces lie buried in the snow;
In passing, their sharp eyes have often snatched
At coral-courts, where rituals unwatched
By any other eye save gull's are kept
By weed-green seamen who have safely slept
Three hundred years a thousand leagues from home.
And after all these marvels still they come,
The feathered faithful, landing on the mere
As heart returns to home, year upon year.

145

WALKING AT NIGHT

Thus I would walk abroad when gentle night
Puts on her friend's cool cloak and bids me come,
Walk among beds of lightly sleeping flowers,
Budded in silver dreams of friendliness.

And I would lie among the dainty herbs,
Like catmint, parsley or exquisite thyme,
To watch the late bird, twittering, hurry home
Across the moon's great watchful eye, to love.

These things, like dreams of princesses and pearls,
Come to me more as iron days grate on;
The brush of blood paints not a ruined world,
But thyme and parsley underneath the moon.

IN THE THIRD YEAR OF WAR

I dream now of green places,
And the gentle kine
Wading knee-deep in rushes;

I dream of singing birds,
And summer rain,
And gracious, homely words.

But I wake to bitter winds,
And blown sand's whine
Across forgotten lands;

And empty skies at night,
And cold star-shine
Where lonely spirits meet.

146

I feel all this, my dear,
Alone, my love, alone
With all the old fear.

I dream now there is no ending,
No golden, breathless dawn;
Only seeking, seeking without finding.

THREE PLEAS

Stand by me, Death, lest these dark days
Should hurt me more than I may know;
I beg that if the wound grows sharp
You take me when I ask to go.

Step closer, Love, and dry your eyes,
What's marred you'll never mend by tears;
Let's finish where the tale began
And kiss away the ruined years.

A moment, Faith, before you leave,
There's one last favour I would ask;
Put to some use your handsome hand
And show me the face behind your mask.

BIRDS

Do they, the little tufted birds,
See the glory of God:

Or weep salt tears to see poor Christ
Bleed on the tree?

Or is the tiny flickering heart
Cold as a hail-stone:

The note we take for lyric joy
Mad requiem of hate?

CIRCLE

The first keen hunter dreamed a fiery rose,
And stumbling through a forest full of eyes,
Had scratched his arabesque across the wall
One second before crumbling rock could fall.

The last pale wanderer watched the hunting bird,
And searched his dying memory for word,
But only found a ghastly flowering flame,
Sour smell of dust, bleak skeleton of home.

POEM

The word that lies inside the head
And never shows its face
Paints coloured snakes of Paradise,
And maidens, soft-limbed in their grace.

The word that's spoken spells decay
And death within the walls,
Like a mad pharos lures the heart
To break on subterranean hills.

148

SYMPATHY WITH STONE

Blood-red the lily, and the questing horn
Shrivelling in silence;
Crumbling the archway, tumbled stone
Trembling at violence
Of rain and frosty ruin and the crushing heel;
No tenderness,
No knowledge of that soul
Which cries in every stone, how hewn, how shaped.

We quarried you and gave you for a name
His title whom you shielded from the wolf,
Who left you standing naked, when his shame
Gave him grave's armour, left him safe
With you to take the punishment, sad stone.
How living among men, how dead alone.
You suffer, I could find my part to weep . . .
But hush, I think this dying stone's asleep.

POEM

Who murdered the minutes,
The bright golden minutes, the minutes of youth?
I, said the soldier, dressed in his red coat,
I with my trumpet, my sword and my flag,
I murdered the minutes.
I took the minutes and what good I did,
For see how the black men kneel, he said.

Who killed the hours,
The gay purple hours, the hours of faith?
I, said the Parson, in his black cloak,
I with my book, and my bell and my pen,
I killed the hours;
I killed the hours as my holy right,
And see how the people kneel at night!

Who slew the years,
The sweet precious years, the years of truth?
I, said the Lover, in her gay gown,
I with my lips and my breasts and my eyes,
I slew the years;
I slew the years, my silly dove —
And see how you kneel to me in love!

POEM

Call me the Twelve of the red rye field
Where the winds of the heart howl white through the night;
Call me the life of the unborn child
That waits like a dog at the gates of Death

For a master who's gone,
For a man who is bone,
And a home where there never can be one.

(So the dead lie deaf and tongueless. Let them lie
Unhurried by the bell that wags our limbs.)

Yes, call me the girl of the golden hair,
With breasts as pert as a sonnet's rhyme;
Or the old man shuddering at the clock,
As he watches his fingers turn to lime

For a God who's stone
And a love that's flown;
And all so afraid of being alone.

(For the berry clacks on the blackened bough,
A thorn in the breast of the starving bird.)

Call, I say, lest the sky should fall
Or mountain slip and cover all;
The Christ must come ere the poem ends,
So call, for pity's sake, O call!

POEM

When quiet comes over the hill again
And light breaks from the door,
Then blond will drink with black again —
But the poor will always be poor.

When trees put on their fruit again
Sweet songs will colour the night;
But though man may sing with other men
The knife will always be bright.

When love comes back to the heart again
We'll pay for bread with faith;
But the gold that will ease the rich man's pain
Will still buy the poor man's death.

THE LANTERN AND THE GHOST

A lantern tumbles me to hell,
The sun is blind to death.
Through dark decay I see my way
Across the midnight heath.

The ghost who totters at my side
Can make or mar my fate;
The strong-armed god of yesterday
Has smiled too late, too late!

POEM

Blood in the bud, born of the unicorn,
The Lord's bright, punished bull, lover of flowers,
And stars, shield of the heavenly host, the light
Of faith on faith advancing to despair,
Blood in the bud, I say, nipped like a worm
Between two lovely sticks where boys have passed,
Man's days between the gestures of a God,
Life cut to ribbons with the knives of love,
Blood in the bud is all we can expect.
From dreams spring up the trees of happiness,
The bold roots thrusting through the soil of love,
Fingering the rocks of living with rude hands,
Teasing the rocks of passion with bent boughs;
From dreams explode the birds that should hold hope,
From tiny rooms of anguish painted green
Where mortal man lies sick a century's span
Waiting for godhead and the golden dawn.
From dreams the flowers fall, shorn by the wind
Of winter when the golden hairs are gone,
And swords lie rusted underneath the hedge.
And so I cite the unicorn, that fabled knight
Prancing through woods, a star pierced by his horn
To light his path among the darkening trees,
Symbol of love, of faith, of courage, and of death,
Youth's gallant charger and the school-boy's dream,
Maker of melody, guide to the land of deeds
That burn their way through all creation's book;
Thus youth remembers and will thrust out buds
That, reddened later by the world's sharp lance,
Shrivel and fester in the horn-hung light.

Y DDRAIG GOCH

The dragon of our dreams roared in the hills
That ring the sunlit land of children's songs.
Red with the lacquer of a fairy-tale,
His fiery breath fried all besieging knights.
Whole seasons could he lay the land in waste
By huffing once upon the standing corn!

He was our dragon dressed in red, who kept
Sly ghosts from lurking underneath the thatch,
And made the hen lay dark-brown eggs for tea.
One word to him, just as you went to bed,
Made Twm, the postman, call next afternoon;
"Ho, bachgen," That is what he'd say, "Just look,
A fine blue postal-order from your Mam!
Twm gets a pint for bringing that, I bet!"

The dragon cured us when the measles came,
And let the mare drop me a coal-black foal.
He taught us where nests lay, and found us fish,
Then thawed the snow to save the winter lamb.

Ho, Ddraig Goch, my pretty, pretty friend!
We were his children, knowing all his ways;
We laid out nightly gifts for him beneath the hedge,
Five linnet's eggs, a cup, a broken whip,
And heard his gracious sighs sweep through the trees.
But tears for all the fools who called him false!
One lad who sniggered fell down Parry's well;
The English Parson had a plague of warts;
Old Mrs. Hughes was bitten by a cat;
The school roof fell in when the teacher smiled!

Ho, Ddraig Goch, they tell me you are dead;
They say they heard you weeping in the hills
For all your children gone to London Town.
They say your tears set Tawe in a flood.

I'm older now, but still I like to think
Of your great glass-green eyes fixed on the Fferm,
Guarding the children, keeping them from harm.

Don't die, old dragon, wait a few years more,
I shall come back and bring you boys to love.

PLAINT

The knife that slew me was a word of love,
A rose still rich with poison's syrup, held
For these white lips to kiss, to kiss the hands
That crept from underneath the coat like claws.
I ran in sunshine like a careless child,
Spending the minutes with a child's delight,
Reckless of leaves that fell before my feet,
Blind to the growing shadow at my side.
When passion broke and spilled its tired tides
Against the crumbling rock, my heart, I woke
And heard the tiny crying of the drowned,
The helpless years I sacrificed to love.

And then I looked to see the failing hand
Still clutched the crackling rose the worm had found.

VICTOR AND VANQUISHED

Heart in purple, body in rags,
Soul among angels, hand among rogues,
And the black thorn-tree that should be a throne,
Piercing like sword to the golden bone.

Come at the midnight, walk with wolves,
Know all the agony spilled blood salves;
Slack down the picture and break the word
And count the gay maggots in dangling bird.

We tortured the world with a peacock's feather,
Conscripted the son and slew the father,
Laughed to see blinded white eyes search
And watered our horses in France's church.

But now the world's a sorry place,
Where each man wears the same dead face,
Each woman bears the same dead child,
As the winds wail wild, so blackly wild.

Oh Father of Swords and Screaming Steel,
Why can we never break the will;
Why must these ghosts smile, slow as Time?
Oh Father, can we not go home?

A NOTE ON THE TYPE IN WHICH THIS BOOK IS SET

The text of this book is set in Caledonia, a Linotype face designed by W. A. Dwiggins. Caledonia belongs to the family of printing types called "modern face" by printers — a term used to mark the change in style of type-letters that occurred about 1800. Caledonia borders on the general design of Scotch Modern, but is more freely drawn than that letter.

The book was composed, printed, and bound by the Plimpton Press, Norwood, Massachusetts. The binding and typographical arrangement are based on original designs by Mr. Dwiggins.